iPhone 11
User Manual

Complete Guide for a Beginner &
Senior on General Uses of iPhone
11 with Upgrading Techniques
&Many Informative Screenshots,
Latest Tips & Tactics

Ephong Globright

Copyright © 2020

Facts Acclamation

This iPhone 11 User Manual is primarily designed to provide complete solutions to several operational challenges on the use of many basic apps, technical setup, ensuring comfortability, and safe usage of the iPhone by the dummies, beginners, and seniors.

Table of Contents

INTRODUCTION

By popular demand on self-explanatory iPhone 11 guide with step by step screenshots and easy to understand tips, I have decided to produce a very clear and simple iPhone 11 manual to read and understand for both a beginner and senior even dummies to become a professional in the use of iPhone 11 effectively.

This iPhone 11 user manual is fully produced to completely provide a total solution to many challenges that may prevent beginners or seniors in the use of many apps available on the iPhone.

It is of a great opportunity to have this straight forward understandable important guide to assist you on how to completely navigate through your newly purchased iPhone 11 and get all that you are looking for quickly.

Many users are actually using iPhone 11 within a limited scope of 20 to 30% benefits of the total 100% benefits loaded in it.

Has it come to the extent of always looking for someone to help you perform simple settings that you should able to do yourself without asking for anyone's intervention?

Anyways, this is because many users only exposed to elementary methods of using the iPhone 11 successfully but not understood the major techniques involved in the working out of step by step activation settings of all the apps features on their iPhones.

Therefore, I had compiled all the basic and advanced steps of becoming a professional of your newly purchased iPhone 11 in this do-it-your iPhone 11 user guide. The user manual contained self-explanatory and informative screenshots, latest tactics, and special tips on every important setting and operation on your iPhone.

First and foremost, there is a need for a user to initially familiarize himself or herself with all the external and internal properties that the iPhone 11 is made up of. This will enable him/her to fully know how to use them correctly.

iPhone 11 is compassionately designed by Apple organization for every individual that deserved a comfortable life which I strongly believed that you deserve it and qualified to use it efficiently.

You must understand that irrespective of your age, whether you are young or aged, still everything about you is superior to the iPhone; therefore, you should be able to operate your iPhone excellently, because the iPhone is primarily designed to serve you and satisfy your specification to the optimal level for you to fulfill your purpose.

In that view, I have used more relevant and important clear pictures and screenshots to buttress my operational illustrations for you to fully know everything about your iPhone.

iPhone 11 Features Fact

Overall Outside Operational Parts of iPhone 11

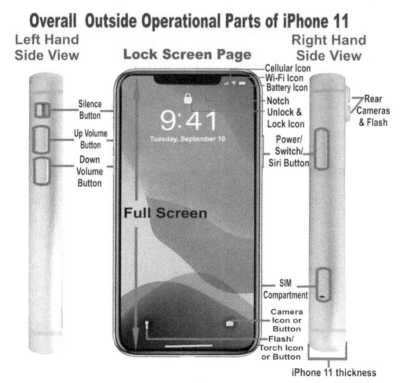

iPhone 11 thickness

To start with, let's look at the general outside operational components of the iPhone 11.

The above picture explained the different locations of finding various important parts that you can use to operate your iPhone 11 with ease. For instance, the SIM Compartment and Power button are located on the right-hand side of the iPhone, while Silence, Up Volume, and Down Volume buttons are located on the left-hand side of the iPhone. The Rear Cameras and Flash are located at the back of the iPhone.

The Important Components In Your iPhone 11
Notch Details

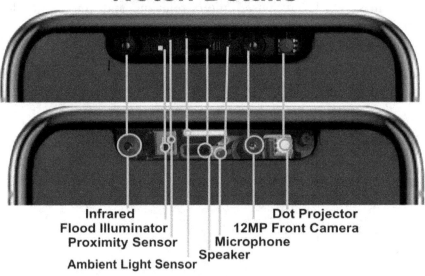

Infrared	Dot Projector
Flood Illuminator	12MP Front Camera
Proximity Sensor	Microphone
	Speaker
Ambient Light Sensor	

Sensors In Notch: The iPhone 11 has Barometer, Three-Axis Gyro, Proximity Sensor, Accelerometer, and Ambient Light Sensor.

Front Camera: This is the camera at the front of your iPhone which is called *Front-Facing Camera*. It comes with TrueDepth of 12MP of a small focus of depth field f/2.2 aperture with a resolution of 4K, 1080p, and 720p HD for Cinematic high video recording and picture capture.

It has a capacity of making 4K video recording speed in 24 fps, 30 fps, or 60 fps with the ability to perform 1080p at 120 fps for Slow motion (Slo-Mo) and has Photo Next-generation Smart HDR.

Rear Cameras: These are the two cameras at the back of your iPhone 11:

1. 12MP Wide Camera with a small focus of depth field f/1.8 aperture.
2. 12MP Ultra Wide Camera of a small focus of depth field f/2.4 aperture.

The two cameras can stabilize optical image with Photograph Next-generation Smart HDR that overcome night interference with the use of Night mode. The rear cameras are efficient to record QuickTake video.

Zoom Magnification: You can zoom out optical images 2 times to the original image on your camera screen and digitally zoom in the image up to three times the original image on iPhone 11. You can also perform Audio Zoom as an innovation in the iPhone generation.

Portrait Mode: The Portrait effect in the Camera capture is an advanced Portrait Mode that can further use to beautify images through Filter and 6 Portrait Lighting Effects which include Natural, Studio, Contour, Stage, Stage Mono, and High-Key Mono.

Audio Playback: You can effectively use iPhone 11 to make Audio Playback with supported Dolby Atmos and Spatial Audio Playback.

Video Playback: The iPhone 11 can be appropriately used with a supported HDR10 Content and Dolby Vision

A13 Bionic Chip Capacity: It comes with A13 Bionic Chip of Third Generation Natural Engine that is boosted with an in-built internal

Random Access Memory of 4 GB to improve the operational functions of the iPhone in term of uploading, execution of various tasks which include setup, video recording, sending or receiving of messages, downloading of video, performing of transaction... and many others.

12 MP Ultra Wide Rear Cameras
Flash
12 MP Wide Rear Cameras
Back Side

Face Scanner | Speaker | Front Facing Camera
Notch
Front Side

6.1 Inches (154.9mm)

5.94 inches (150.9mm)

2.98 inches (75.7mm)

iPhone 11 Dimension: The breadth (width) of the iPhone 11 is 2.98 inches or 75.7mm by 5.94 inches or 150.9mm of Height; the weight is 6.84 ounce or 194g; The thickness 0.33 I inches or 8.3mm.

XDR Display: The iPhone 11 screen is uniquely designed with Extreme Dynamic Range (XDR) of Liquid Retina HD display which is the advance level of ordinary High Dynamic Range (HDR) to provide the optimal clear, distinct attractive neutral color and real images to resolve poor background and boost actual image display.

iPhone 11 comes with a diagonal liquid Crystal Display (LCD) Screen size of 6.1 inches of general screen Multi-Touch with In-Plane Switching Panel (IPS) Technology.

Variable Storage: iPhone 11 come with different storage capacities of 64 GB, 128 GB, and 256 GB (Gigabyte) that determine the price of the iPhone 11. The storage capacity is the space that is naturally available on your iPhone. The more the space capacity the more data or documents you can store on your iPhone storage. Therefore, if you go for iPhone 11 with high storage capacity you will have an opportunity to have more data or documents on your iPhone, however, you can still complement your iPhone storage with iCloud Storage to backup all your data and apps on your iPhone 11.

Battery Durability: iPhone 11 has a very strong and long-lasting battery capacity to enable you to perform long activities. It is 1hour stronger than iPhone XR Max. The longevity of the iPhone 11 is sufficient enough for you to perform any power-consuming activities on it.

iPhone 11 Battery

Although, on many occasions, the rate of battery discharge depends on many activities you are performing on your iPhone 11 and the duration of time you use to do them. If you are doing many functions or using the iPhone in a longer time than usual without being recharged, it may reduce the battery durability.

> ➢ **Video Playback:** iPhone 11 can closely last 17 hours to make Video Playback. But for streamed video playback, it will last about 10 hours.
> ➢ **Audio Playback:** At a stretch, your iPhone 11 could endure 65hours in making Audio Playback; what a fantastic durable satisfaction.

Rate of Battery Charging: In 30minutes your iPhone 11 is capable of charging up to half of the whole battery. This implies that the time taking to charge is drastically smaller to the rate of time taken to discharge.

Battery Maintenance Facts:

1. When you have fully charged your iPhone 11 battery, remove it from the source of light before you start operating the iPhone.
2. Ensure you have used the battery to 40-30% charged before you connect it to the source of electricity to recharge your iPhone 11's battery.

3. Always avoid your iPhone 11 battery from being completely discharged or rundown to 5 or 0% before you recharge it.
4. Do not allow the iPhone 11 to suddenly trip off because the battery has been totally discharged before you start charging it.
5. Set the battery percentage limit and battery protective mode on your iPhone to provide your iPhone longer time usage.
6. If you want to carry out a setup or uploading or downloading or recording on your iPhone and it will take too much of time which the current battery power level cannot complete, immediately, connect it to the source of electricity to boost the battery capacity and once it is fully charged then disconnect the iPhone 11 from the Lightning to USB cable and continue your activity.

The Charging Connection of iPhone 11 with Lightning to USB Cable and Adapter

In the package of the iPhone 11, you will see a Lightning to USB Cable, an Adapter of 18 Watt, a Pair of Earpod with a connecting Cable, and a SIM Card Tray Ejector.

iPhone 11 Charging Connection

Power Port
Power Connector
First End

Lightning USB Cable

Second End

USB Adpter Connector

USB Adpter

First Step: Take the first end of the lightning to USB Cable and insert it into the iPhone Power Port under the bottom of the iPhone 11.

Second Step: Take the second end of the lightning to USB Cable and insert the USB connector into the USB lightning adapter port at the head of the Adapter.

Third Step: Plug the USB Adapter pins inside an electric Plug socket and switch on the button of the plug.

14

Hint: Within a few seconds the charging battery with the percentage charged will show on the screen for you to know that the iPhone 11 is perfectly charging. 53% Charged But, if you waited for about a minute without you seeing the charging battery icon come up, adjust the adapter connects with the main plug of the source of electricity.

Available & Compatible Wireless & Cellular: iPhone 11 is compatible with EDGE or GSM, DC-HSPA, Gigabit-class LITE, HSPA+, or UMTS, few models of CDMA EV-DO Rev. A, Bluetooth 5.0, Preserving Power of Express Cards, In-Built of GNSS or GPS, 802.11ax Wi-Fi 6 with MIMO and NFC with reader mode.

IP68 Certification for Water, & Dust Endurance: iPhone 11 has just a 30-minute resistant ability to endure 2 meters of water depth. It is not advisable to deliberately put your iPhone 11 in water that you do not know the depth of the water. It is only satisfied with the 2-meter depth of water not more than that. More also, the iPhone 11 can survive in a dusty environment.

Documents You Can Access on Your iPhone 11

There documents you access on your iPhone 11 without looking for a format converter. Any of the accepted documents can be used or shared on the website page, mail, social media platform or to compose a message on your iPhone as a reminder or planner… and many others.

The documents are:

1. Microsoft Excel of XISX and XIS
2. Microsoft PowerPoint of PPTX
3. Microsoft Word of DOCX and DOC
4. Text of TXT
5. Image of JPG, GIF, TIFF;
6. USDZ Universal of USDZ, ZIP, and ICS
7. Keynote of KEY
8. Preview and Adobe Acrobat Document Format of PDF
9. Contact information of VCF

10. Rich Text Format or RTF
11. Numbers of NUMBERS format.
12. Web Pages of HTML and HTM

GUIDE ONE

How You Can Use Compatible Protective Accessory on Your iPhone 11

Despite the fact that Apple company has just planned drag out sturdy iPhone 11 external ringside to fulfill the user's want by utilizing a stainless glass body to prevent water and to enable quick removing of stain when it is fallen into a gumming stain or dust.

Yet, it is not sufficient for those that need the iPhone to be completely ensured from any accidental condition that may damage the fragile screen of the iPhone.

Apple organization just gave limited security, not an absolute guide that could forestall the iPhone 11 screen from harm when it unexpectedly falls on a hard pointed surface. Therefore, it is wise of you to give a more reliable extra Screen Protector and quality body Casing on your iPhone.

Presently the decision of giving outright security to your iPhone 11 depends on you. On the off chance that you are searching for where you could get a quality and strong iPhone 11 body case or screen protector, I can recommend the Amazon platform.

On Amazon.com there are numerous quality and keen iPhone body Case and Screen Protectors that will likewise add magnificence to your iPhone look. At the website homepage click on the searching field and type *"iPhone 11 Case"* or *"iPhone 11 Screen Protector"*.

Many quality products will display, look for the product with excellent reviews, or Tagged Amazon Bestseller. Most importantly read through the existing reviews of the product you want to buy to learn from people's comments.

17

How to Place Screen Protector without Bubble on the Screen

In the package of a few iPhone protectors, you will two sachets which one of the sachets is called Wet Wipe while the second sachet is called Dry Wipe.

Materials You Need:

Alcohol Swap, or Isopropyl Alcohol, Microfiber Cleaning Cloth (MCC) (e.g., Magicfiber, e-cloth,), Dust Removing Sticker (DRS), Thick Paper Business Card

First Method

1. Switch off your iPhone
2. Use alcohol swap or add small Isopropyl alcohol into clean cotton to clean up the surface of the iPhone screen to remove oil on the screen surface. Ensure you clean from inside to the edges of the iPhone.
3. Use the available MCC to clean the iPhone screen surface from edge to edge to completely remove dust.
4. Use a side of DRS to sweep the screen surface from the top to the bottom of the screen. Just 2 to 3 times (Optional).
5. Remove the protective paper/nylon at the front of the Screen Protector.
6. Gently hold the Screen front the left and right sides with your hand.
7. Slowly bend down the head of the Screen protector toward the head of the iPhone. Use your second hand to support the screen protector at the opposite end to align the screen protector edge with the iPhone top edge.
8. Slowly move your hand holding the screen down; with the help of the thumb of the second-hand press the screen surface to remove any possible bubble and use the Thick Card to slightly press the screen down and sweep the surface toward the bottom of the iPhone side by side as you are moving down your hand to prevent bubble(s).

Second Method

1. Remove the protective nylon or paper on the screen protector surface.
2. Position the side of the screen protector at one side of the iPhone to ensure that the screen is at the center of the iPhone. Some screen protectors come with tape stickers but if you do not have never mind.
3. Position the upper end of the screen protector at the same upper end of your iPhone XS or XS Max and gently move down your hand until it gets to the opposite end.
4. Allow it to spread and use the Microfiber Cleaning Cloth to press the screen surface from the top of the iPhone by moving your hand from left to right till you will get to the bottom of the iPhone to prevent a bubble. Or

Third Method: Nylon or Paper Sticker Support Method

➤ If you have a paper sticker, cut three of 4cm of paper sticker each. Stick 2cm from the length of the paper sticker at the left, right, and bottom center.
➤ Gently position the screen protector top edge at the exact top edge of the iPhone screen.
➤ Look at both sides, and ensure the screen protector is aligned with the iPhone edge.
➤ Use the remaining 2cm paper sticker at the left and right to adhere to the screen protector with the main iPhone body.
➤ Hold the opposite paper sticker to slowly bring down the screen protector to the surface of the iPhone XS or XS Max.

Use clean soft MCC to rub the surface of the protective screen from left to right to prevent bubbles as shown in the below pictures.

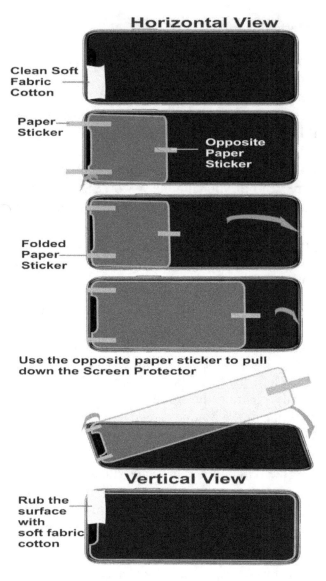

How To Position & Insert Recommended SIM Card on iPhone 11

Acceptable SIM Cards for iPhone 11: Micro-SIM cards could not be used with your iPhone 11, but you can use nano-SIM and eSIM. However, in the event that you are having any of the satisfactory SIM cards, you can feel free to insert it for it will surely work.

iPhone 11 SIM Card Insertion

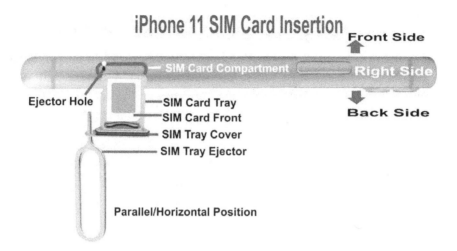

There is a **SIM Tray Ejector** in the iPhone 11 pack that you will use to eject the SIM Card tray from the right-hand side of the iPhone below the Power Button.

First Step: Let the front of your iPhone 11 face-up; pick up the Ejector and let it be equal/flat to the hole at the lower end of the SIM Card tray as it is shown in the picture above.

Second Step: Put in the SIM Ejector into the small hole to touch the end surface inside and push the surface, promptly, the SIM Card tray will halfway come out.

Third Step: Use your hand to pull it out completely.

Fourth Step: Let the Circuit Steel surface (the front face) of your SIM Card face up and place the card on the tray according to the shape of the SIM designed on the tray. Try not to place the SIM card against the shape designed on the SIM Tray. Try not to flip around the SIM face.

Fifth Step: Put the SIM Tray with SIM Card into the SIM compartment as you removed it. Now you are good to continue the next line of action.

The Special Method of Solving Problems

The uncommon methods of tackling issues in this iPhone 11 User Manual are remarkably masterminded in basic manners that will enable you to effortlessly use or make the right steps in accomplishing an ideal answer for any operational issue.

I have given simple to-do ways to deal with search through the whole suggested application' icons or orders from either the lock screen or home screen to the specific spot that you would accomplish your points.

Personally, I separated all the gradual steps to enable you to understand "what you will do at every point", "after the point and what you will do next".

Although, several authors preferred writing operational steps in what I called **Condensed format**. For instance, if you want to enable **Live Photo** on your iPhone in a Condensed format, it will be written as **Settings** < **Camera** < **Preserving Settings** < Switch On **Live Photo.**

As a beginner, this method will be difficult to get his or her mission fulfilled unless there is someone to guide him through.

But, in this manual, all the operational techniques are self-explanatory steps.

At first, the page that you will see what you are looking for was mentioned. The name of the page was written in red bold fonts e.g. Homescreen, Settings, Apple ID, Camera, Contact… and many others.

Let's take the above steps for the activation of **Live Photo** in what I called condensed format as an example in my comprehensive format.

Homescreen: Hit on the **Settings App** icon (first line of action)

Settings: Scroll down and hit on the **Camera** icon (Second line of action)

Camera: Select **Preserving Settings** (Third line of action)

Preserve Settings: Hit on the **Live Photo** activation switch to change to green.

On the first line of action, you will see Homescreen appears in red bold color which means the page name, while **Settings App** appears in a bold black font which means "what you are looking for on the page (i.e. your mission)".

On the second line of action, the **Settings App** changes to Settings because at this stage you have launched the Settings page, and on the page, you will see **Settings** at the top of the page therefore the red color appearance of Settings is representing the Settings page not "mission", while **Camera** is your next mission on the Settings page.

In the third line of action the bold black font **Camera** changed to bold red font Camera, this is to tell you that you are now on the Camera Page and you will be looking for **Preserving Settings...** and when you hit on it you will see **Live Photo** to activate and the Preserving Settings will become the name of the page.

Meaning of Common Terms (Words)

Please get used to the meaning of the below simple terms I used in this book to help rapid learning and digestion of different technical steps.

Hit or **Select**: This means **"Tap"**. Whenever you see hit on a particular **application** or **feature**, I mean you should tap on the app or the feature.

Activator: It is used for the "switch button" to turn on apps features in Settings. ⬅️ or ⭕

Activate: This means you should turn on the **Activator**. ⭕

Deactivate: This means you should turn off the **Activator**. ⬅️

Regulator: It means **"Control"**. It has a round button on a parallel line that can be moved to either right or left to regulate the level of volume of a sound or light on your iPhone 11 Settings.

Type: It means "Enter" words or numbers into a text or searches filed.

Text or Search Field: This is a place where you can type in words or numbers

GUIDE TWO

How You Can Know Details of All Important Features on iPhone 11

Lock Screen Features Importance

Lock screen: There are numerous speedy functions you can perform to fulfill your need without you going to Homescreen to do them. The helpful features are *Timer, Notifications, Touch, Camera, Apps, and News Searching Tool, Control Center, Padlock, Battery Charged Level, Network Strength Bar, Wi-Fi Indicator, and Cellular Service Provider's Name.*

The most significant features you can deal with and work on them are:

Timer: It self-adjusts with the most precise local worldwide period of your area. It instantly determines locational timing.

Notifications: It strictly works by your instruction to determine the information that will be shown on the Lock screen.

But, by default, it could display all information about calls, emails, messages, alerts, and alarm notification. However, you may prevent the showing of your messages or mail detail from the Lock screen in the notification settings to protect your information from being read by others.

You have to unlock your iPhone before you can be able to perform the following:

Flash: You can use the flash at the bottom left of the Lock screen to lightening the dark environment and facilitates sharp and clear output of pictures taking in uniformly dark surroundings.

Camera: It can be constantly used to perform video image capturing and pictures taking without you navigating through the Homescreen.

You could swipe from the right side of the iPhone to launch the Camera page or press the Switch button to access Camera and click on any of the down or up buttons for volume at the left side of the iPhone to take the shot if you don't want to use Shutter on the Camera interface.

Apps Searching Tool: When you slide your iPhone from the left side you will see searching tools that will enable you to find many apps information about your iPhone. Ask more of Apple store, iCloud, or Siri to have full knowledge of them. There is much informative news that is displaced below that you can hit on to read details.

Place your finger at the bottom of the Notch frame center of your iPhone and slightly move down your finger you will see a searching field with suggested favorite Apps that you can navigate to get what you need on the iPhone.

But, if that app you are looking for is not among the suggested apps, you can further type in the app into the searching field to access the app.

Hint: Whenever you see **Search or Text Field** on your iPhone without seeing any Keyboard to type text into the field. All you need to do is to initially hit on the surface of the **Search or Text field**, immediately Keyboard will appear below for you to enter your search text keywords into the field. Examples of apps that contain text field are Mail, Messages, Safari, or other Browsers,

Camera, Call Contact, Calendar, FaceTime, Health… and many others.

Control Center: You can view Control Center from the Lock screen. Swipe down from the right side of the Notch at the center top of your iPhone.

How You Can Know Different Apps & Their Function on Homescreen

Mostly, all features available on the Lock screen can be effectively performed on the Homescreen; even more can be done directly.

You can repeat the side screen and the Notch frame center searching methods on the Homescreen.

Several icons are available for you to navigate on to ease your smooth findings and operational functions. The individual app name is mentioned below as they were arranged row by row in the Homepage picture above.

This is the list of various applications (apps) that are available on your iPhone 11 with iOS 13 are *Messages, 9 Calendar,* *Photos,* *Camera,* *Weather,* *Clock,* *Maps,* *FaceTime,* *Notes,* *Reminder,* *Stocks,* *News,* *Home,* *iTune Store,* *Apple Store,* *Books,* *Health,* *Wallet,* *Settings,* *Podcast,* *Phone,* *Mail,* *Safari,* *Music,* *Find My,* *Shortcuts,* *Contacts,* *Compass,* *Measure,* *Calculator,* *Files,* *Watch, and* *Tips.*

You can still request more apps on your iPhone through Apple Store freely. More apps you can get from the Apple store are *iMovie, iTunes Remote, iTunes U, Number, GarageBand, Clips, Keynote, Pages, and Music Memos.*

All the above apps are very important for you to fully benefit the operational efficiency of your iPhone and make life very simple to explore and achievable. **The most important and inevitable Apps that you must know the beneficial features are: Settings, Call, Messages, Camera, Photo, FaceTime, Siri, Safari, Mail, and Music.**

Settings: This app will enable you to access the settings of all the available apps on your iPhone. Through the Settings app, you can perfectly activate all the essential apps (e.g. Face ID, Siri, Passcode, Wi-Fi Network, iCloud, etc.) that you are unable or skipped during your iPhone setup.

Phone: This will enable you to reach out to your friends or loved ones that you are having their **contact** details on your iPhone. The phone app will enable you to receive and make a call.

Massage: This will enable you to send text messages to your loved ones in your contacts. You have two ways of sending a message to people.

1. SMS or MMS
2. iMessage

SMS or MMS: You can send a text message through SMS and MMS to anyone on your contact that is using an Android phone. The sending button is green

iMessage: This is a live interactive message medium that will enable you to see when the person you are sending your text message to is typing his/her messages. It is only available for those who are using an iPhone. The sending icon is blue.

Camera: This will enable you to take new pictures or images and record videos of any event. In it, there is image beatifying features that can be applied to edit and modify the image output.

Photos: In this app, you can fully access all your saved pictures regarding time, day, month, location, and event. This app will arrange and indicate the source of store images such as *Screenshot, WhatsApp, Facebook, Video, Movies, DCIM, Camera, Live Pictures…and others.* You can add labels to any specific event photographs.

FaceTime: As the name of the app implies **FaceTime,** it will enable you to make face to face calls, audio calls, live to chat text messages on your iPhone with the use of the latest Animoji or customized, Memoji and Emoji.

Siri: This app is a wonderful work-executor and apps, problem solver. It serves as a messenger or personal assistant to help you determine several activities associated with other apps on your iPhone. It can help you set and save time in Alarm, a reminder for events, check daily weather/climatic condition, recall the missed calls or messages and it can also help you compose messages and send to whosoever you want to send it to.

If you call its attention, it will do anything you want it to do for you. Its voice could be set to female or male voice all depends on your choice. It is one of the great successes ever apple has achieved in using technology to solve the iPhone user's bothering issues with ease.

How to talk to Siri

Safari: This app is used to browse for any information online or to download more applications, games, dictionaries, music, videos, language translator, WhatsApp, Facebook… and many others.

Mail: The App will enable you to instantly access your received email messages and to reply to messages.

Music: This app will enable you to play any audio music in your music library.

Health: This is an amazing App that you can use to track everything about your health to ensure your daily general wellbeing. You can also use it to monitor your daily food consumption through the regulation of calories and monthly menstrual cycle in women; heart condition, fasting discipline, sleeping status, working ability... and many other activities essential to your comfortable life.

Find My: This is App very important to either quickly use to locate your misplaced iPhone or retrieve suspected lost iPhone without using a Wi-Fi network or Cellular connection even when the battery is done you can still recover your lost iPhone.

Now that you have familiarised yourself with all the essential Homescreen apps' icons and the most inevitable apps' features, then we have to move further on how you can apply their features and how to activate their functions through Settings.

How You Can Prevent Ringtone, Notification Alert, and Vibration

There are two major ways on your iPhone that you can use to prevent calls from ringing out or to avoid vibration or notification alert or alarm sound.

External Buttons

Silent Mode Button: The silence button is first button you will see on the left side of the iPhone. The small button could be moved from the front of the iPhone to the back direction of the iPhone.

Once you push the silence button backward from the front of the iPhone the floor front space will show red color as it is shown in the diagram.

Immediately silence notification will appear at the top center of the screen **"Silent Mode On"**. This means that you have muted the iPhone, therefore, there will be no sound from a call, alarm, and notifications but it will vibrate if you have previously activated vibration during settings.

But, when you move the button from the back to the front of the iPhone the ring sound, alarm and notification alert sound will restore (i.e. unmute).

Push the Button Backward to Activate Silence Mode

Left Side of iPhone 11

Do Not Disturb

Lock Screen or Homescreen: Swipe down the screen from the top right side of your iPhone notch.

Do Not Disturb Icon: Hit on the **Do Not Disturb** feature to prevent ringtone and vibration from any call, message notification, alarm, and alert sound.

How To Initially Put Do Not Disturb Into Action

You will perform this in Settings to make the feature to be effective on your iPhone.

Homescreen: Hit on the **Settings** icon

Settings: Search down for **Do Not Disturb** and select it.

Do Not Disturb: Hit on the activator button to change to green.

Schedule Time You Don't Want To Be Disturbed By Anyone

If you schedule the time you do not want people to disturb you with calls or messages then the above option (Do Not Disturb) will be deactivated automatically because you cannot use both features at the same time. You have to choose one.

Schedule: Hit on the Schedule, to set the time you don't want people to disturb you.

Specify Those Favorites That Your iPhone Can Allow

You have to choose some specific favorites that must be excluded from **Do Not Disturb** instruction. The **Favorite Contacts** maybe your Spouse, Children, Mother, Father, and Close Relative that may seek your attention unexpectedly should in case of any unforeseen Emergency.

Allow Calls From Hit on **Allow Call From** to select your favorites by tapping on the **Favorites** option.

Repeated Calls: Hit on the **Repeated Calls Activation Switch** to allow regular calls of your chosen favorites when you are busy till you pick it.

Activate: Hit on **Activate** to select **Manually** from the three available options which they are:

1. Automatically
2. When Connected to Car Bluetooth
3. **Manually**

Manually you will always be able to activate **Do Not Disturb** through Control Center.

Auto-Reply To: Select **Auto-Reply** to choose the **Favorites** and **Auto-Reply Message** that will explain why you can not pick-up your iPhone presently.

How To Make Your iPhone Sleep & Wake

Ii is good to always use sleep and quick wake mode on your iPhone, because while you are working on the iPhone at any page you may want to temporarily shot down the screen to rest and later come back to the work.

You could instantly make use of the sleep and wake button to return to **Lock Screen** without you passing through the vigorous steps of backing the page one by one through "**Back**" or "**Home Swipe Up**"

Click the **Power/Switch Button** on the right side of the iPhone. Just a click the screen will go black meaning sleep and when you make a click again on the same **Power Button** the iPhone will awake at the **Lock Screen.**

Meanwhile, any of the security authentications like Face ID or Passcode may probably require. If your Face ID failed your Passcode will be automatically displayed for you to enter.

Auto-Sleep

Your iPhone may sleep automatically if the idle time (the time you are doing anything) has passed the time frame you set in the Settings of the iPhone screen activities, therefore, your iPhone will sleep. Wake the screen by clicking the **Switch Button** to wake it on the same page you have stopped working.

How to Move App's Icons from a Place to Another on Homescreen

It is very easy to rearrange all the apps on the Homescreen by moving each app to the place you prefer on the screen. You may choose to arrange the apps in alphabetical order or base on the regular use or importance of the

apps.

Homescreen: For a short time press the screen for an optional box to appear.

Optional Box: Hit on the **Rearrange Apps** option. Immediate the entire apps will be stirring and unstable with the *Cancel sign* attached to the left top angle of each app.

Apps: Position your hand on each App you wanted to move and drag the app to the favorite place. As soon as, you are through with the rearranging of the Apps as you wanted then **Swipe Up** the screen from the bottom.

How to Keep Two or More Apps in a File on Homescreen

Homescreen: For a short time press the screen for an optional box to come up.

Dialog Optional Box: Tap on the **Rearrange Apps** option. Immediate the entire apps will be stirring and unstable with the *Cancel sign* attached to the left top angle of each app.

Apps: Position your hand on an App and drag it on another app to have the same file. Before you release the dragged App on the below App make sure that a transparent white square appears around the below app. You will see the File Name text field above, hit on the text field to name the file.

If you want more than 2 Apps in a file, then continue dragging Apps on the file you have created and hit on the external part of the file to restore and fix it.

As soon as, you are through with the rearranging of the Apps as you wanted then **Swipe Up** the screen from the bottom, the whole apps will come back to normal.

How to Return the Apps to the Previous Position

Created File

> ➢ **Two Apps in a File,** hold-down the file for an optional box to show up for you to tap on **Rearrange Apps.** Immediately, the two Apps will be released from the file and show as an individual app on the Homescreen.
>
> ➢ **More than Two Apps in a File,** hold-down the file to show an optional box for you to tap on **Rearrange Apps** and all the Apps will be liberated.
>
> ➢ **If you want to be taken the Apps out of the file one after the other:**
>   - ✓ Hit the file compartment the whole Apps will be seen boldly.
>   - ✓ Place your finger on any of the App and drag it out. The file will contract back while the liberated App will be in its normal side.
>
> ➢ **Swipe up** from the bottom to stabilize the apps.

35

How You Can Select Wallpaper for Both Lock Screen & Home Screen

On your iPhone, you can change the default Wallpaper to another lovely self-picture or different designed images that will make both Lock Screen and Home Screen looking more pretty. The Wallpaper is sectioned into four categories:

1. Dynamic Wallpaper
2. Still Wallpaper
3. Live Wallpaper
4. Photo Wallpaper

Dynamic Wallpaper: The wallpaper contains several circular bubbles in different sizes that slightly increase in size on the screen.

Still Wallpaper: The wallpapers comprise of different designed stable images and natural picture without movement.

Live Wallpaper: Once you touch the Wallpaper it will start moving. Any image that is chosen in this category for your either Lock screen or Homescreen moves when you press down the screen. You can preview the animation before you set it for either the Lock screen or Home screen.

Homescreen: Hit on the **Settings** icon.

Settings: Scroll down of the page and select (hit/tap) **Wallpaper**

Wallpaper: Above the Lock Screen and Homescreen Image hit on **Choose A New Wallpaper.**

Choose: You will see Dynamic, Still, and Live galleries in a row with the series of your photo events arranged in the column below.

➢ Hit on any of the Wallpaper options provided or your customized personal photo.

➤ Hit on a Set option below the **Wallpaper**. But, if you do not like it, you may select **Cancel** to take you back to Wallpaper Choose page to re-choose wallpaper.

➤ Optional Box will display three possible options that you may separately consider. There you can choose any of these options **Set Home Screen, Set Lock Screen,** or **Set Both.**

Set Home Screen: The Wallpaper you have chosen will only appear on Home Screen.

Set Lock Screen: The Wallpaper will only show on the Lock Screen.

Set Both: The Wallpaper will show in both the Lock Screen and Home Screen. Therefore, you can choose two different Wallpapers for the two screens (i.e. Home & Lock Screens).

How You Can Delete Apps on Homescreen

Homescreen

➤ Hold-down the app until you will see an optional dialog box.

➤ Hit on the **Delete** option. Immediately the app will be removed. *OR*

➤ Hold-down the app till you will see the whole app stirring and unstable with Cancel indication at the left angle the apps.

➤ Hit on the **Cancel sign**. Immediately the app will be removed from the page and the whole apps will automatically rearrange themselves.

➤ **Swipe Up** to stabilize the apps.

Homescreen Smart Tactics

This will effectively protect your iPhone 11 from experiencing sudden uncontrollable stiffness, abnormal movement of the screen, hanging off the screen, self-switch off… and many others.

1. Make sure you completely close all the open pages on your iPhone when you finish using it.
2. Anytime you want to use your iPhone for long period make sure it is fully charged.
3. Enable "Low Power Mode" to prolong the battery time on your iPhone when the energy remain is 50%.
4. All the moving effect on your iPhone will stop working when the battery is very low which include the Live Wallpaper you have chosen on your Lock screen or Home screen.

Total Close of Opened Pages at the Homescreen

Homescreen to Lock Screen: Swipe down the left side of the Notch of your iPhone, alternatively place a finger at the center of the Notch bottom frame, and swipe down the screen toward the bottom of the iPhone. The Lock Screen will show.

How to Reduce Open Pages into the App icons on the Homescreen

Homescreen

> Hit on two-three different apps' icons on the Homescreen.
> Place your finger at the bottom center of the screen of the page.
> Slightly move up your finger for a small distance and take off your finger from the screen. You will see the app's page entering the app icon on the Homescreen.

How to See the Reduced Apps' Pages

Homescreen (Middle Screen Expose)

> Move up your finger from the bottom center of the iPhone screen and slightly move it in an inverted seven Γ direction.

- As your finger is moving toward the right side of the iPhone you will see those open pages coming out from the left side of the screen.
- You can hit on any of the reduced opened app pages you still want to revisit to work on or get more information from.

Homescreen (Bottom Screen Expose)

- Place your finger on the first end of the horizontal Homescreen Bar at the bottom center of the iPhone and move your finger to the second end of the parallel bar.
- As you are moving the finger the page will be coming out one after the other. You can move from right to left or vice versa.
- Hit on any page you are looking for and it will fully display on the screen of the iPhone.

How to Remove the Reduced Apps' Pages

Page Pressing Down Method (after the exposed steps)

- When you press down the reduced open apps one by one for a while, they will show a **Remove Sign** of Minus a circle of red at the left top edge of their pages.
- Hit the **Remove** sign to complete delete the reduced page(s).

Swiping Method (after the exposed steps)

- Place a finger on the individual reduced open app and swipe up further to completely remove the page from the iPhone.

The complete removal of the reduced opened pages on your iPhone regularly will prevent your iPhone from a drastic slowdown of the iPhone speed efficiency.

How You Can Activate Low Power Mode To Increase Battery Duration

The use of battery mode on your iPhone will enable you to use your averagely charged battery three times longer than usual battery strength.

When you have set the battery mode on your iPhone to be active at a 50% charged level of the battery, it will actively reduce many apps that are internally using the battery abnormally. However, the brightness of the screen light will be regulated according to the level of brightness you have set for **Low Power Mode** in the settings.

The Live Wallpaper will stop working when battery mode is active.

Activate Through Settings

Homescreen: Hit on the **Settings Icon.**

Settings: Move down the page to hit on **Battery**

Battery:

➢ Hit on the **Low Power Mode** to be activated by changing the button to Green.
➢ Go back to the Home screen by backing the pages or swiping up from the bottom center of the iPhone.

Activate Through Control Center

You can quickly activate the **Low Power Mode** Manually if you have customized the control through settings. If you want to know how to customize control, go to Guide Three and read how to **add more of the Apps' controls in the Control center**.

Homescreen/Lock Screen: Place your hand at the

right side of the Notch above and swipe down to launch **Control Center.**

Control Center: Hit on **Low Power Mode** icon to activate the feature on the iPhone. The icon surrounding will change to white and the battery charge level will be yellow if it is activated.

How You Can Enable Battery Auto-Lock Control to Improve Battery Life-Time

Your iPhone can lock automatically after a few minutes you have stopped using your iPhone. Before your iPhone could do that you have to go to the Settings on your iPhone to select the time your iPhone should wait after you have stopped using it.

However, if you do not like the auto-lock option you may select "Never" under the available options.

➢ 30 Seconds
➢ 1–5 Minutes

Homescreen: Hit on **Settings Icon.**

Settings: Gently move down of the page to select on **Display & Brightness.**

Display & Brightness

➢ Hit on the **Brightness** activating switch to become Green.
➢ As you have activated the switch the Brightness regulator will be active. Then Move the Brightness regulator toward the left to reduce the light intensity.

Night Shift: If you have not activated the **Night Shift** hit on it and put it "ON". After you have activated it, go to the Control center to deactivate it by pressing down the **Screen Light Control** (Brightness control) and hit on **True Tone.**

Auto-Lock: Hit on the Auto-Lock to select your preferred time that you want your iPhone to remain active when you are doing anything.

Rise to Wake: Put "On" the activator, so that you may hit your iPhone screen when it is about to sleep.

Text Size: If you are not satisfied with the font size of the whole text on your iPhone you can go ahead and hit the **Text Size.** Move the Knob regulator toward the right to enlarge the text size on your iPhone screen. But, If, it is already too large, you can then move the knob regulator toward the left. (Optional)

Bold Text: You can make all the text on your iPhone screen to appear bold if you are not satisfied with the current look of the text font on your iPhone.

Hint: If you alter the text size or bold text, it will surely affect all the words on your iPhone.

GUIDE THREE

How You Can Manually Setup your iPhone 11 after Purchase & Start Working

There are many needful things you have to make available before you can start the setup of your iPhone as a First timer. In the event that you are formerly using Android telephone and now you need to begin using iOS (iPhone Operating System), initially you need to make your iPhone 11 connect with Cellular Service Provider Network or functional Wi-Fi Network.

You will also enable your Bluetooth at the control center. All these will help you to transfer your data and documents on an Android phone easily.

Everything you will do to accomplish your purpose on your iPhone 11 is systematically discussed in this manual.

For senior iPhone user, that has been using the lower iPhone model before and now want to move to an advance generation of iPhone model; you can start your iPhone 11 setup manually if you know that you do not have much important data or documents to transfer from the old Android that you may later transfer through data transferring method if you choose to do.

But, if you virtually want all your data and documents on the old iPhone to be completely transferred into the new iPhone 11 you will need to follow the automatic transferring setup of iPhone 11 that will be discussed after this manual setup with other important procedures that you must strictly follow to successfully set up your iPhone 11.

What To Do First

➤ When you removed the iPhone 11 from the sealed pack, connect the lightning to the USB cord to the power port at the under bottom center of the iPhone.

➤ Connect the other USB end to 18 Watt USB port adapter at the head and plug it into the electric source to charge the iPhone.

➤ If you are having a Computer, you can connect the USB connector of the cable to your fully charged Computer USB port.

➤ On the iPhone screen, the current battery charged will appear. Once it is fully charged disconnect your iPhone 11 from the source of electricity.

➤ Put in your SIM card according to the method you have been told earlier under *Guide 1*.

➤ Protect the iPhone casing with a nice iPhone 11 case and screen protector.

Do you have videos, audio music or messages, photos, or any other essential documents you want to transfer from your Personal Computer or Android Phone?

➤ Turn On the Wi-Fi network on your Android or PC containing the data or documents you wanted to transfer into your new iPhone 11.

➤ Rename the Wi-Fi ID on your Android or Computer Wi-Fi settings to ease the recognition on your iPhone 11. (Optional).

➤ Ensure that the Network is active and your Android or PC is fully charged.

iPhone 11 Manual Setup Begins

You can now manually set up your newly purchased iPhone 11.

1. Power Switch Button
   Look at the right side of the new iPhone you will see a button, Press down till you will see a big **Hello** font interpreting in different languages on the screen

2. Hello
   Swipe up from the bottom center to tap on your **Language**.

3. Select Your Country or Region
   Scroll down to tap on your **Country.**

4. Quick Start
   Look down the screen hit on **Set Up Manually.**

5. Choose a Wi-Fi Network
   Hit on the name of your **Wi-Fi Source.**

6. Enter Password
   Enter the correct password of the **Wi-Fi Network** and tap on **Join** at the top right side of the screen.

7. Data & Privacy
   Hit the **Continue** bar

8. Face ID
   a. Hit on the **Continue** bar.
   b. Hit on the **"Get Started"** bar
   c. Focus your eyes on the Front-Facing

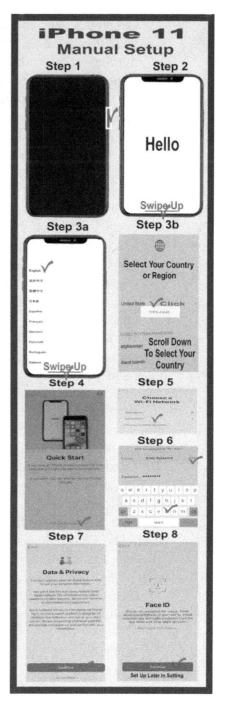

45

Camera Sensor and let your head be in the middle of the round frame on the screen.

d. As you are turning your head gradually the surrounding lines of the round frame will be changing to green, keep turning your head and let every side of your head be captured by the Camera sensor till the surrounding lines are completely changed to green.

e. If the Face ID is successful, a **Continue** page will display. Hit the **Continue** bar.

9. For later Face ID Settings hit the second option **Set Up Later in Settings.**

10. Create a Passcode
Use the Keypad to type a complex **Passcode.** But, if you are not prepared, then tap on **Passcode Options** and hit on **Don't Use Passcode.**

11. Passcode Box
Hit on **Don't Use Passcode.**

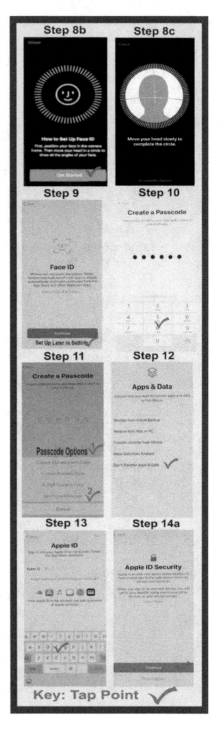

46

12. **Apps & Data**

If you are having data on Android Phone you can hit on the option **Move Data from Android. Other options**

a. Restore from iCloud Backup

b. Restore from Mac or PC

c. Don't Transfer Apps & Data

13. **Apple ID**

a. Tap on the Text Field, use the Keyboard to type your Email address

b. Hit on **Next** at the top right angle side.

c. Type a correct **Apple Password** inside the text field.

d. Hit on **Next** at the top right angle side.

14. **Apple ID Security**

Hit the **Continue** bar to register your **Phone Number.**

But, if do not want that to be done during setup then you tap on

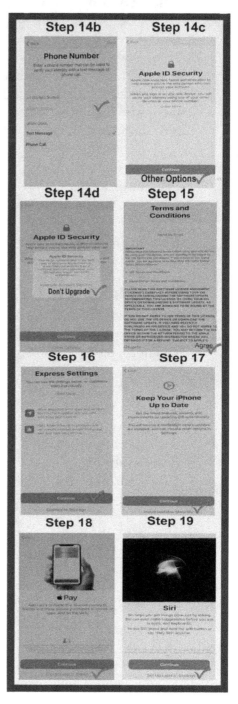

Other Options
Hit on **Don't Upgrade** on the **Request Box.**

15. **Terms and Condition**
Read through the terms and conditions that are required of you on how to successfully use your iPhone and follow them strictly. Tap on the **Agree** option at the downright area of the screen.

16. **Express Settings**
Hit **Continue** bar below

17. **Keep Your iPhone Up to Date**
Choose the below option of **Install Update Manually.**

18. **Apple Pay**
Enter your Apple Wallet detail if it is available with you by hitting on the **Continue** bar.
But, choose **Set Up Later in the Wallet** option below, if you don't have.

19. **Siri**
Tap on the **Continue** bar to register Siri (optional)
But, tap on **Set Up Later in Settings** to perform the full settings of Siri through the Settings process.

20. **Screen Timer**
Hit **Continue** bar (optional), it could be done later, therefore, for now, choose **Set Up Later in Settings.**

21. **Apple Analytics**
Select the **Don't Share** option below Share with App Developers.

22. **True Tone Display**
Hit on the **Continue** bar

23. **Appearance**

a. Select on the **Light** option to make the iPhone screen appear brighter.

b. Hit **Continue** bar

24. Display Zoom
Hit **Standard** small circle to select it.
Hit **Continue** bar

25. Go Home
Hit **Continue** bar

26. Switch Between Recent Apps
Hit **Continue** bar

27. Quickly Access Controls
Hit **Continue** bar

28. Welcome to iPhone
Swipe up from the bottom middle of the screen to access the **Homepage.** If you create a Passcode during setup, the iPhone will ask you to enter your registered Passcode before you can launch into the Homescreen.

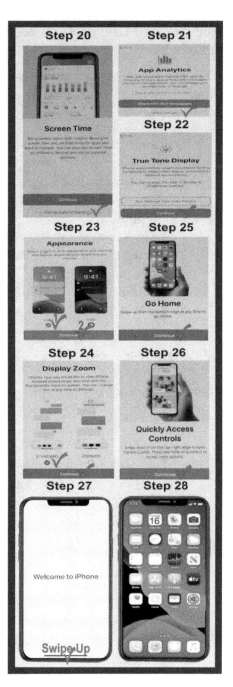

For Android User to Transfer Data and Vital Document s into iPhone 11

You need to upgrade your formal data and documents on your Android phone for you to have the latest details on your iPhone after the transfer.

- ✓ Ensure that your Android Phone Battery and iPhone Battery are 100% charged.
- ✓ Use a strong Wi-Fi Network and turn On your Bluetooth. Alternatively, you can initially do the manual setup of the new iPhone 11 for you to use the new iPhone 11 Hotspot Wi-Fi Connection on your Android that will make the transfer to be easy and successful.

Take these steps on your old Android Phone

Homescreen

- ➢ Hit on Google Play Icon.

Google Play

- ➢ Hit on Google Play at the top of the page
- ➢ Use Keyboard to enter **Move to iOS** and tap on the suggested Move to iOS keyword dropdown.

Move to 1OS Interface

- ➢ Hit on **Open** bar
- ➢ Do not hit on **Continue** until you are on the page of Apps & Data where you will first hit on **Move Data from Android**

On your iPhone 11

1. Click the **Power button** on the right side of the iPhone 11.
2. Swipe Up the **Hello** page from the bottom and select your **language** (e.g. English).

Select Your Country or Region

1. Scroll down to select your Country by tapping on it.
2. Allow it to complete the **Setting Language...** processing.

Quick Start: Hit on **Set Up Manually.**

Choose a Wi-Fi Network: Select the exact **Wi-Fi network** you are using.

Enter Password:

1. Type the **"Password"** for **the Wi-Fi** correctly into the **Password Text Field.**
2. Hit on **Join** at the top right of the page.

Data and Privacy: Hit on **Continue Bar**

Face ID: Hit on **Set Up Later in Settings.** If you have not done the Face ID.

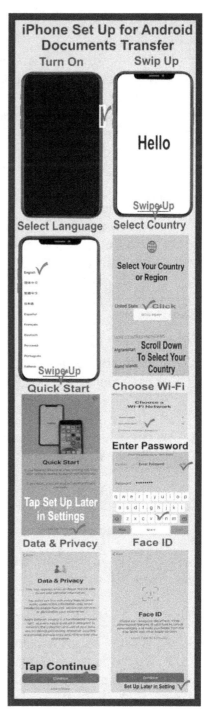

51

Create Passcode:

1. Hit on **Passcode Options** and select on a dialog box **Don't Use Passcode**. It is optional, you may create the Passcode if you want to.

2. On another dialog box showing that "**Using a Passcode is Highly Recommended**" select "**Don't Use Passcode**" again to continue.

Data and Privacy: Hit on **Continue Bar**

1. Face ID: Hit on **Set Up Later in Settings.** If you have not done the Face ID.

2. Create Passcode:

3. Hit on **Passcode Options** and select on a dialog box **Don't Use Passcode**. It is optional, you may create the Passcode if you want to.

Apps & Data: Hit on **Move Data from Android.**

➡ iOS Move from Android

➢ Hit on **Continue** below
➢ Type the "**Code**" that shows on the screen of your iPhone into your Android phone.

On Android Phone

52

Move to iOS

> Hit on **Continue** above the iOS phone image.

Terms and Conditions

> Hit on **Agree**

Find Your Code

> Hit on **Next** at the top angle of the screen.

Enter Code

> Use the Keypad to enter the **Code** on the iPhone into your Android Phone.

Transfer Data:

> Select all the documents or data that you wanted to send from your Android to your new iPhone.
> Hit on **Next** at the top corner of the screen.

If you have taken too much time before you enter the code into your Android Phone the transfer may be impossible.

If you experienced an unsuccessful transfer,

immediately, hit **Back** at the top left of the iPhone screen and re-tap on **Continue** to get another code. Enter the code fast into your Android Phone.

As soon as the transfer is complete on your new iPhone then tap on **Continue Setting Up iPhone.**

Continue your iPhone setup steps from Step 13 above to complete the iPhone setup.

How You Can Automatically Transfer Data & Apps from Old iPhone into A New iPhone 11

To Start With

What you must get ready before you can start the manual processing of moving your important documents or data to your new iPhone.

- ✓ Charge your old & new iPhone battery to 100%
- ✓ Make cellular data available on your old iPhone
- ✓ Switch On Wi-Fi Network and Bluetooth on your old iPhone.
- ✓ Position the two iPhones vertically beside each other with a space of 2 to 3 cm between them.
- ✓ Insert functional nano-SIM or eSIM (optional)
- ✓ Apple ID (optional)

What Could Make the Moving of Data to be Impossible Through Manual Setup

Correct the below conditions on your old iPhone before you start the automatic setup:

- ✓ Off Bluetooth or Bad Rear Camera Sensor

✓ Poor Cellular connection or Wi-Fi Network
✓ Entering of Incorrect Apple ID
✓ Activation of *"Find My iPhone"* Settings.
✓ Low Charged Battery

What You Must Do On Your Old iPhone

✓ Recharged your iPhone Battery
✓ Enable Bluetooth
✓ Enable Cellular connection & Wi-Fi Network
✓ Enable *"Find My iPhone"* Settings.
✓ Ensure you enter the correct Apple ID when it is needed.

Note: Low Storage Space (it make slow down the speed)

Starting Approach on the Old iPhone

 There is a need for some little steps of apps' activations through settings on your old iPhone before you continue to move all the data and documents into the new iPhone 11.

The first things to do on your old iPhone are:

➢ Go to Control Center on your iPhone, tap on the Cellular Service icon, Wi-Fi icon, and Bluetooth icon to turn them on.

If the Wi-Fi network is not responding or you have not turned on the Wi-Fi connection on your old iPhone before, then do the following step to activate your old iPhone Personal Hotspot.

Homescreen: Tap on Settings Button

Settings Page: Tap on Personal Hotspot

Hotspot Page:

1. Hit on the **Personal Hotspot** activation switch ⏦ to turn green.

2. On a displayed Wi-Fi and Bluetooth are Off Box tap on **Turn On Wi-Fi and Bluetooth.**
3. On displayed Bluetooth Off Box tap on **Wi-Fi and USB Only.**
4. Hit on Wi-Fi Password

Wi-Fi Password:

1. Hit on the Password Text Field surface and use the keyboard below on the page to enter your **"Wi-Fi Password"**.
2. Hit on **Done** at the top angle of the iPhone.
3. Hit on the Home button to return to Homescreen.
   But, if your old iPhone is iPhone 11 above then swipe up from the bottom.

Now that the old iPhone Wi-Fi Network, Cellular Service, and Bluetooth are turn on and active. Now, you can move to the next stage of moving data from the old iPhone to your new iPhone 11

.

How You Can Protect Your Old iPhone for New iPhone 11 to Recognize

It is advisable for you to initially save all your data in a secured iCloud storage backup by navigating through:

Homescreen – Hit on the **Settings** icon

Settings – Hit on your **Name Profile**

Apple ID – Hit on **iCloud**

iCloud – Search downward and hit the **iCloud Backup** activation button to put on the iCloud Backup.

Backup – Hit on **Back Up Now** to start the iCloud Backup.

Home Button – Click on the round Home Button down to go back to Homescreen immediately. Now you can start the setup process below.

How To Position Old iPhone Beside New iPhone

You can either position the old iPhone on the right side of the new iPhone or the left side of the new iPhone, but what is very important is that they should not be too far from each other.

If you are a lefty/left hand user you can position the new iPhone at the left side of the old iPhone.

But, if you are a righty/right hand using person, position the new iPhone at the right side of the old iPhone because you will perform more installation tasks on the new iPhone than the old iPhone.

Make sure that the distance is 2 to 3cm between each of them.

You may put your SIM card later but make sure the battery is 100% charged before you start.

In this cool guide, I transferred data and apps from iPhone 6 running with iOS 11 to my newly purchased iPhone 11.

Hint: You must upgrade your old iPhone iOS to 11 to facilitate the transfer of the data and document.

Start The New iPhone Automatic Set Up Approach

1. Positioning
   ➢ Place both old and new iPhone beside each other on a table.
2. Old iPhone
   ➢ Unlock the old iPhone and let it be on Homescreen.
3. New iPhone
   ➢ Press the switch button to "On" the new iPhone.
   ➢ Swipe up Hello, within a second your new iPhone will be seen on the screen of the old iPhone.
4. Set Up New iPhone **(Old**

58

iPhone)

➢ Under the new iPhone's image hit the **Continue** bar.

➢ Within a second a round white shape Camera space will show up for you to capture the moving circular eruption.

➢ Take the old iPhone above the new iPhone, let the rear Camera focus on the moving circular eruption, to be viewed in the center of the round space on the old iPhone above.

➢ Hold on till you will see **Finish on the New iPhone** on the old iPhone before you will return it to its formal position.

While the old iPhone is transferring the information into the new iPhone then go to the new iPhone to continue.

5. Enter Passcode of Other iPhone (New iPhone)

➢ Type the Passcode of your old iPhone without making a mistake. Setting Up Your iPhone will show on the screen. Wait till you will see Face ID.

6. Face ID

➢ Hit on the **Continue** bar.

➢ Hit on **"Get Started"** bar

➢ Focus your eyes on the Front-Facing Camera Sensor and let your head be in the middle of the round frame on the screen.

➢ As you are turning your head gradually the surrounding lines

59

of the round frame will be changing to green, keep turning your head and let every side of your head be captured by the Camera sensor till the surrounding lines are completely changed to green.

➤ If the first Face ID scanner is successful, hit on **Continue** bar and move your head in either the same or opposite way, once the second Face ID scanner is complete another page will show and tell you that "**Face ID is Now Set-Up**"

➤ Hit on **Continue** bar

7. Face ID (If you do not want Face ID)

➤ For "later Face ID Settings" hit the second option **Set Up Later in Settings.**

8. Transfer Your Data

➤ Tap on **Transfer from iPhone.** If you have updated all your apps and data, you are good to go.

➤ You may also choose **Transfer from iCloud** if you are very sure that it is up to date. You may tap on **Other Options** to select any other device like Mac, PC, etc.

9. Terms and Condition

Read through the terms and conditions that are required of you on how to successfully use your iPhone and follow them strictly. Tap on the **Agree**

option at the downright area of the screen.

10. Settings From Other iPhone

➤ Hit on the **Continue** bar to proceed.

11. Keep Your iPhone Up to Date

➤ Choose the below option of **Install Update Manually.**

12. Apple Pay

Enter your Apple Wallet detail if it is available with you by hitting on the **Continue** bar.

But, choose **Set Up Later in the Wallet** option below, if you don't have.

13. Apple Watch

➤ Tap on **Set Up Later** under the continue bar to proceed**.**

14. Apple Analytics

Select the **Don't Share** option below Share with App Developers. The next interface will show you how the data is moving from your old iPhone to the new iPhone.

15. Old iPhone

When all the data are completely moved into your new iPhone 11, it will show on the interface of the old iPhone that "**Transfer Complete**".

Hit on the **Continue** bar to enter the Homescreen of your old iPhone.

16. New iPhone

The New iPhone will show Apple's image on the screen. After a while, it will change the screen face to a white interface. Swipe Up

61

the screen from the bottom center and launch into the data loading Apple image interface on the new iPhone 11.

You have to endure enough to allow all the data and apps to absolutely moving from old iPhone to new iPhone because the uncompleted Apps will appear black with a faded icon image on the Homescreen. You will only see the icons that are completely loaded on your screen as they have appeared on your old iPhone.

How You Can Upgrade your New iPhone 11 of iOS 13 to Latest iOS Version

It is of great advantage to upgrading the current iOS 13 on your iPhone 11 to the current version of iOS,

This will enable you to enjoy more newly introduced features on your iPhone 11 and it will improve the general performance in terms of quick execution of uploading, downloading, video recording, browsing network, Animoji customization, automatic backup update, Siri modification, Health tracking or Phone lost tracking efficiency… and many others.

Things You Must Put In Place Before You Get Started

➢ Get an effective Wi-Fi network.
➢ Confirm the available storage space on your iPhone 11. If you do not have up to 90 GB you can purchase from the iCloud store for more storage.
➢ Use iCloud or Mac or PC to back up all the data and documents on your iPhone.
➢ Charge your iPhone 11, and Mac or PC. You may connect your iPhone or upgrading device to a power source overnight.
➢ Make your Password available.
➢ Good lightning to USB cord.

How to perform Backup and iOS Upgrade on Computer

The Operational System for Apple Macintosh Computer (Mac)

➢ macOS Catalina 10.15 or

➢ macOS Mojave 10.14 or lower version.

Note: You may use a PC (Personal Computer) instead if you do not have Mac.

If your Mac is running with a low version of macOS Mojave you can quickly update your Mac by taking the following step on your Mac.

On App Menu:

➢ Select **System Preferences** (operating system).
➢ Click on **Software Update** to look for an Updates
➢ Click on the **Update Now** option to install the latest version benefits. If you select **More Info** you will see full information on the individual update and later choose the one you preferred.
➢ Leave it for a while to completely install till you will see a message that "**your software is up to date**.

Now you can confidently move on to the update process of your iPhone 11 on your newly updated Mac.

Step by Step of iPhone 11 Update on macOS Catalina 10.15

➢ Put On your Mac.
➢ Put On the Wi-Fi network connection on your Mac or PC

➢ Launch **Finder**

But if you are using a Mac running with macOS Mojave 10.14 or less, you will open **iTunes**

Step by Step of iPhone 11 Update on macOS Catalina 10.15

➢ Use the lightning to USB Cable to connect your iPhone 11 with Mac USB port.

- Look at the left side of the Finder page you will see the image of your iPhone and the iPhone name under **Location.**
  - (If you have signed up your name with Apple ID, your first name will appear at the front of the iPhone image). Hit on the name of your iPhone.
  - The location at which you can locate your iPhone varies from the iTunes version to another iTunes version in macOS Mojave and PC.
  - However, the location of your iPhone 11 on iTunes 10 – 12 was shown on the screenshot below.
- Once you click on your iPhone 11 the Update provisional page for your iPhone will display on the right-hand side.
- Initially click on **Back up all the data on your iPhone to this Mac.**
- Click **Check for Update.**
- Click **Download** and **Update.**
- When you are asked to provide your **Passcode,** immediately type your **Passcode.**

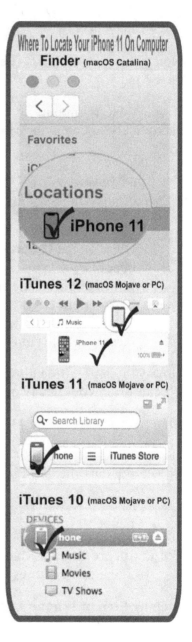

The update will start, endure until the update is complete. Do not interrupt the update processing.

How to perform iOS Update on your New iPhone 11

Homescreen:

➢ Place your finger at the top right of the iPhone screen and swipe down to launch **Control Center.**

➢ Hit on Cellular Service and Wi-Fi network.

➢ Swipe up from the bottom or hit the down plain of the screen to return to Homescreen.

➢ Hit on **Settings Icon.**

Settings: Scroll down to hit on **General**

General: Hit on **Software Update.**

Software Update: Select **Download** and **Install**

If your passcode is required then continue by:

Passcode: Type the correct **Passcode.**

Terms and Conditions: Select **Agree** at the lower left to progress but if you mistakenly select **Disagree** it will discontinue the upgrade.

Immediately, the Upgrade will start, and you can let the iPhone upgrade overnight to completely finish the general processing because it always requires much time.

GUIDE FOUR

The Total Benefits of Control Center

When you get to the Lock or Home screen you can launch Control Center that has all the important icon commands of many amazing features that you can quickly enable to correct and enable the function of several applications on your iPhone.

iPhone 11 has many applications that you can customize through Settings to add them to the Control Center for you to quickly enable.

Majorly by default the following apps and operational icons are in your Control Center:

- ✓ Airplane Mode
- ✓ Cellular Service
- ✓ Wi-Fi Network
- ✓ Bluetooth
- ✓ Music Panel
- ✓ Screen Lock Rotation Icon
- ✓ Do Not Disturb
- ✓ Screen Mirroring Icon
- ✓ Screen Light Control (Contains True Tone & Night Shift)
- ✓ Volume Control
- ✓ Flash
- ✓ Timer
- ✓ Calculator
- ✓ Camera

Airplane Mode Icon: It is used to keep your iPhone out of cellular service or network activity when you are on the Airplane board. It is activated when you hit on the icon surface.

Cellular Service Icon: It is used to activate the cellular service network provided by your SIM cellular provider. Hit on the surface of the icon to see the name of the network provider and active bar at the top left of your iPhone.

Wi-Fi Network Icon: This is a network data-using service that could be activated through **Personal Hotspot** in the Settings or received from an external device like iPhone/Android, Mac, iPad, or PC hotspot via Wi-Fi connectivity.

Bluetooth Icon: This is used to receive or transfer any app data or document from, or to other Bluetooth supporting devices. Hit the surface of the icon to activate the function. You can use it to send sound from your iPhone to another **Bluetooth** supporting sound device to play the sound aloud. You can send one document at a time.

Music Panel: You can use this to play and regulate the sound volume of music from your *YouTube* or iPhone music sound. Hit on the surface of the *Play Panel* to control the sound.

Screen Lock Rotation: This will prevent your iPhone screen display to instantly move from portrait to landscape at any quick repositioning of the iPhone to the landscape. Hit the icon to permanent the portrait screen display but if you want to use your iPhone to watch the **video** you can re-tap the icon to deactivate the effect.

Do Not Disturb: You can use it to stop your iPhone from ringing, vibrating, and notifying you when you are in an important gathering, meeting, on the Airplane board, or driving a car.

Screen Mirroring Icon: This will enable you to see what is on the screen of your iPhone on your Mac, PC, Projector, or TV through the use of a specific cable connector. Hit the surface of the icon to set the device connection and activate the application.

Screen Light Control: It is used to control the brightness and dimness of the screen light. If you want the screen light to be brighter, put your finger on the bright region of the control and move your finger up. But, if you want the screen face to look dim or dark move your finger from up to down.

When you press down the control **Night Shift** and **True Tone** will appear below the screen.

You can further change the mode to **Night Shift** mode that will change the screen appearance to yellowish-cream like the evening period to protect sight (eyes).

Although by default (i.e. from the factory) it is set to **True Tone**, the icon activation appears blue.

Volume Control: It is used to control ring tone, alarm, video, or audio sound volume on your iPhone. Place your finger on the surface of the volume icon and high the volume by moving up your finger or low the volume by moving down your finger.

Flash Icon: It is used to "On" **Touch/Flashlight** at the back of your iPhone. If you hit the **Flash icon** once immediately the Flashlight will display for you to see clearly or to make the back environment of your iPhone look like daylight and aids quick search.

Timer Icon: It is used to set various **Timer** formats and display the Timer on the **Homescreen.** Once you hit on the **Timer** icon you will access every detail of **Timer Setting.**

Calculator Icon: It is used for adding, dividing, subtracting, and multiplying numbers in mathematical calculations like mathematician, accountant, statistician, or everyone, and it can be extensively changed to a scientific calculator for a scientist to calculate advance calculation. Hit the **Calculator** icon for it to appear.

Camera Icon: It is quickly used to access a **Camera** page for you to take pictures and make videos. Tap on the Camera icon to get into the page instantly.

How You Can Add Apps' Controls in Control Center

Customize Apps into Control Center

Homescreen: Hit on **Settings Icon.**

Settings: Move down the page and hit on **Control Center**.

Control Center

> ➤ Hit on **Customize Control**.
> ➤ You will see **Access Within Apps**, put the activation button On if not activated by hitting on the activator.
> ➤ Hit on **Customize Control**.

Customize Control

> ➤ You will first see those controls that are in the Control Center listed above with a red circle having minus (remove) at the center that can be used to remove any of the controls from the Control Center if you deliberately hit on it.
> ➤ More listed Controls below are the available controls that you can add to those apps controls in the control center when you hit on the green circle having a cross sign (add) at the center. These are some of the controls you can add with those I have previously mentioned above:

Accessibility Shortcut, Apple TV Remote

Alarm, Magnifier, Text Size, Note,

Guide Access, Do Not Disturb While Driving,

 Low Power Mode,  Voice Mail,  Stopwatch... and many others.

> Keep tapping on the **Back** icon at the top-left region of the iPhone to return to Homescreen or **Swipe Up** from the bottom to return to Homescreen.

How You Can Create & Check Your Customized Controls from Control Center

View Controls on Lock Screen or Homescreen

> Place your finger at the top right side of your iPhone and swipe down

You will see the additional controls below those controls I have mentioned above.

If you do not see it, go back to Settings again to confirm if the control is still among the list of **Add More.** If you see it among the list, then hit on the **Add Circle** at the front of the control Icon to add it.

If it is not among **Add More** but among the list of those that are already in the control center then revisit the control center by swiping down the screen of the iPhone from the right side. Search carefully you will see it there.

70

How You Can Enable iPhone Screen Brightness from The Settings

Homescreen: Hit on the **Settings Icon**.

Settings: Scroll down of the page to hit on **Display & Brightness** to access the settings.

Settings: Hit on the **Brightness** activation slide to become green.

➢ Slide the Brightness adjuster from left to right to elevate/high the screen light or you slide the adjuster from left to right to reduce the screen light.

How To Enjoy The Beneficial Features of iTunes App on Your iPhone 11

iTunes app is an important tool in terms of adding more pieces of stuff to your iPhone through your PC by sending and getting more pictures, music, video, etc. on your iPhone.

iTunes Store could be used to download many videos or music and play them offline on your iPhone with the use of a Wi-Fi connection. However, the service does not go free of charge, that is, you will pay for every music or audio requested at the iTunes store.

Syncing your iPhone with iTunes to Improve Feature Benefits

These are the following items you can add (sync) to iPhone from your iTunes library:

➢ Playlist,
➢ Movies
➢ Songs

- ➢ Podcasts
- ➢ Album
- ➢ Photo & Video
- ➢ Audiobooks
- ➢ Contact & Calendars

You should sync your iPhone with iTunes if you want to include the below items on your iPhone:

- ➢ **iTunes Playlists** but you will initially subscribe with **iTunes Match or Apple Music.**
- ➢ **Personal Video**
- ➢ **Calendars, Photos,** and **Contacts** provided you are not using **iCloud.**

You can also use iTunes to delete the formally added items from your iPhone.

All those lively benefits can be downloaded from the iTunes Store without you passing through the PC connection.

For you to get the iTunes Store App on your iPhone freely by using Password take the following step.

Homescreen

- ➢ Hit on **Settings Icon**

Settings: Hit on your Name or Sign In and select the **iTunes & App Store.**

iTunes & App Store: Hit on **Password Settings**

Password Settings

- ➢ Switch on Face ID for buying all you need.
- ➢ Below PURCHASE AND IN-APP PURCHASE hit on your desirable requirement (what you need).
- ➢ Below FREE DOWNLOAD you will see **Require Password**, hit the activator to become Green.

➢ As soon as, you are requested to provide your **Password,** then enter it.
➢ Hit on **OK.**

How To Use Your iPhone 11 to Send Audio Sound into AirPlay Speaker

Homescreen: Go to **Control Center**

Control Center: Hit on **Screen Mirroring** icon

Screen Mirroring: Press the **Audio Card** down for a few seconds and the **AirPlay** icon should be tapped on.

AirPlay Speaker: Hit the **AirPlay Speaker** to be connected.

How You Can Get Video and Music Through Different iPhones to Your iPhone 11

Settings on your iPhone and the other iPhone

Homescreen

➢ Go to **Control Center,** put On **Bluetooth** and tap the screen, or swipe up from the bottom center to go back to the Homepage.
➢ Hit on **Settings**

Settings: Select (tap) on **General**

General: Hit on **AirDrop**

AirDrop: Select **Everyone** and swipe up for Home or continually tapping on the **Back icon** at the top left of the screen till you get Home.

For iPhone Sending Video and Music (i.e. the iPhone Sending Video and Music)

Homescreen:

➢ **Videos**

73

- ✓ Hit on **Photos Icon** to pick on a Video you want to select the video.
  Or
- ➢ **Music**
  - ✓ Hit on **Music Icon** and select your preferred music.
- ➢ Hit on **Share Icon**
- ➢ Select **AirDrop** by tapping on it.

On Your iPhone

- ➢ Tap on **Accept** in the optional notification of **AirDrop.**

On iPhone Sending Video and Music

- ➢ Hit on your iPhone Name you are sending items to.

Instantly the new iPhone would receive the selected item.

Use Emergency Call to Prevent Unforeseen Danger on Your iPhone 11

You need to get used to quick ways of activating emergency provision and the quick approach of making the call when you noticed experience danger or around you that may result in loss of treasure or life if you do not get expert attention urgently.

Switch Button: Click the **Switch Button** 5 times.

Homescreen: Hit on the **Settings Icon.**

Settings: Move down to hit on **Emergency SOS**

Emergency SOS: Hit on **Also Works with 5 Clicks.**

Anytime you noticed a sudden attack or unforeseen danger, all you need to do is just to click the Switch Button 5 times and instantly you will be connected to **Emergency SOS.**

Other Method

Press down **Switch Button** and **Up Volume** together for the **Emergency SOS** screen to show up.

At the center of the screen, you will see **SOS Switch.** Slide the **SOS** Switch from left to right side to be connected to Emergency Call.

Hint: You can also switch off your iPhone on the same page by moving **Power Switch** from left to right.

Why You Need App Store on Your iPhone 11

You can fully download several apps and interactive social applications like Instagram, WhatsApp, Facebook, iMovie, Numbers, Keynote, Pages, GarageBand... and many others through the Apple store.

Homescreen: Hit on the **App Store** icon

App Store: Hit on the **Continue** bar.

Browsing Page: On a request optional box showing on your screen, tap on **Don't Allow** for Apple store not to access your location.

App Search: Look down the lower left side of the screen to hit on **Search Icon.**

> Hit the search field to type in your app request.
> As soon as you seen the App below, hit on "**Get**" at the opposite for instant **Download**.
> Make Home **Swipe Up** to see the new App Icon.

The Complete Settings of Notification

Homescreen: Hit on the **Settings** icon.

Settings: Move down and hit on **Notification**

Notification: Hit on the **App Store**

App Store: Give commands to your iPhone by activating the provided options that are including **Allow Notification, Badge App, Show on Lock Screen, Show in History, and Show as Banner.**

> ➢ Hit on any of these options below:
>> ✓ **Temporary Banner Show**
>> ✓ **Persistent Banner Show**
> ➢ Make Home **Swipe Up.**

For Your iPhone Notification Preview

It is optional for you to choose where you want the notification preview to be shown when the iPhone is locked or unlocked. After the above steps, hit on the **Back** icon for Notification at the top left of the screen to return to the **Notification Page.**

Notification: Select **Show Preview**

Show Preview: You may select **Always When Unlocked or Never.** But for confidentiality you may tap on **When Unlocked**, that means, it only you can see the notification(s).

How to Protect Your Cellular Data to Last Longer

The use of LOW DATA MODE reduces the level at which all the apps using data to function on your iPhone.

Homescreen: Hit on the **Settings**

Settings: Select **Cellular**

Cellular: Opposite **Cellular Data** hit on **Roaming Off.**

Turn On the activation switch of **Low Data Mode** to green.

Technical Approach for iPhone Freezing or Malfunction

In any situation, you observed that your iPhone suddenly stopped working by not responding to touch and you could not open the app(s) on your iPhone then take the following steps to restart your iPhone.

Stop working at any page you are on your iPhone

Left Side of the iPhone

- ➢ Click **Up-Volume** button
- ➢ Click the **Down-Volume** button.

Right Side of the iPhone

- ➢ Use 11 seconds to press the **Power Switch** button.
- ➢ The iPhone Switch Off and reboot itself to Lock Screen.

Lock Screen

- ➢ Home Swipe Up.
- ➢ Provide your **Passcode**
- ➢ Home Swipe Up.

GUIDE FIVE

How You Can Track Your Health Correctly on Your iPhone 11

This will enable you to sincerely examine your health wellness by launching the Health App and recording all your health histories in the Health App to see the complete exercises information that is created on your iPhone and the various applications you have used up to the period you are checking the health data.

With help of the Health App your day-by-day distance running exercise, gradual physical steps, walk, sleep, mental stability, fertility status, diets, weight balance... and several others could be automatically tracked. If you are also having Apple Watch, you could perform the same function of tracking your daily activities and generate relative data to compare with the previous days.

Additional information and the record could be achieved the following Apps: Workout, HealthFit, MySwimPro, Runtastic, Gymaholic, MyNetDiary, iSmoothRun, ManMyRun... and more other Sources that are helping you in organizing your daily activities and execution of health projects or budgets daily, weekly, monthly, or yearly.

Exceptionally, a heart condition, menstrual cycle... and others require the use of the Apple Watch with your iPhone 11 running with iOS 13 and above to get the accurate record and full benefits of more of the innovativeness and efficiency loaded in the Health App.

What To Do First

You will need to provide your Medical Details in these three profile sections:

1. **Health Profile:** It contains your Name, Contact, Date of Birth, Sex, Blood Type, Fitzpatrick Skin Type, and Wheelchair.
2. **Medical ID:** It shows the same Emergency information on your iPhone or Apple watch which also contains activation of Emergency when your iPhone is Locked, Date of Birth (DOB), Medical Conditions, Medical Notes, Allergies & Reactions, Medication, Blood Type, Organ Donor, Weight, Height, and Emergency Contacts.
3. **Organ Donation:** This will enable you to register for an Organ donor through the **sign up with Donate Life.** It comprises the following data of yours; Names, DOB, Last 4 Social Security Number (SSN), Email, Address, ZIP, and Sex.

How You Can Set Up Your Health Profile

The setup of the Health App is slightly different from iOS to iOS. If your iPhone 11 is running with iOS 13.1 the welcome process will be a little different from the starting process of iPhone 11 that is upgraded to the latest iOS 13.5.

However, all you need to do is very simple; just promptly follow through the welcome steps as they come up on

79

your iPhone Health Page.

But the major setup processes (steps) of registering your essential profile to make the Health App active and do what you wanted will be fully discussed below.

Health App Setup Steps:

Homescreen: Hit on the **Health App** icon.

Health: Hit on **Summary Tab**.

Summary: Hit on your **Profile Picture** at the top right side of the page.

Your Name Page: Hit on **Health Profile**

Health Profile:

- ➢ Hit on **Edit** at the top right angle of the page.
- ➢ Provide your Age, Weight, and Height
- ➢ Hit on **Done** at the top right angle of the page

How You Can Set Up Medical ID

Homescreen: Hit on the **Health App** icon.

Today Page: Hit on the **Medical ID icon** at the right bottom of the screen ✳

Medical ID: Hit on the **Create Medical ID** bar.

✳ Medical ID

- ➢ Hit on **Show When Locked** activation slider to enable to access Emergency when your iPhone is locked.
- ➢ Hit on **Add Photo** to upload your photo on the page
- ➢ Hit on **Add Date of Birth:** You will see the date suggested at the bottom of the screen. Scroll up until you will get to your Month/Day/Year and hit on it to select.

80

- ➢ Hit on **Medical Condition** to type your health discomfort (e.g. Herpes, Stomach ache, Arthritis, etc.).
- ➢ Hit on **Medical Notes** to write medical history.
- ➢ Hit on **Allergies & Reactions** to write the signs and symptoms in the text field. I do not have any reaction you may write "Nil/None".
- ➢ Hit on **Medication** to write the doctor's prescription on the text field. If you do not have, you may type "Nil/None"
- ➢ Hit on **Add Blood Type** to select.
- ➢ Hit on **Organ Donor** to select "No, Yes or Not Yet"
- ➢ Hit on **Weight** to select your body weight
- ➢ Hit on **Height** to select your height.
- ➢ Hit on **Add Emergency Contact** to select your trusted loved ones' contact from your iPhone contact list. You can add many favorite contacts.
- ➢ Hit on **Done** at the right top angle of the screen.

To Confirm How The Emergency Settings Work
- ➢ Press the **Power** Button to sleep and re-press the button to wake the iPhone.
- ➢ Use your Face ID to unlock the iPhone.
- ➢ Swipe up from the bottom

81

center of the screen to see the lock screen with the **Emergency** at the bottom left of the screen.

➤ Hit on the **Emergency**

➤ **Emergency Call:** If you must access Medical ID, then hit the **Medical ID** at the bottom left of the screen. All the information you have provided during the setup.

➤ At the bottom of the Medical ID page, you will see the **Continue bar**. Hit on the **Continue** bar to complete the registration.

➤ Hit on **Complete Registration with Donate later** bar.

➤ **Thank You:** Hit on the **Done** bar.

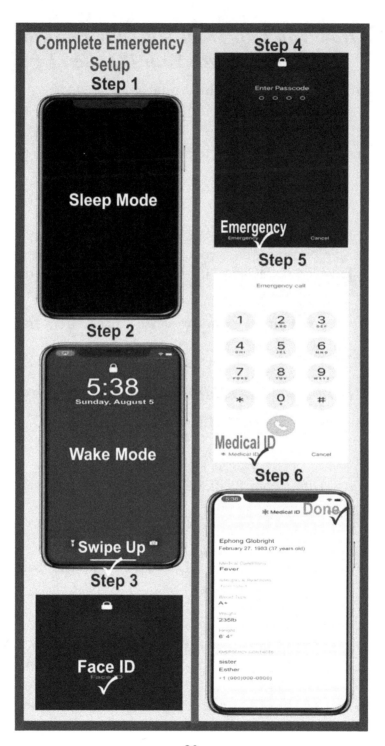

How You Can Track All Your Favorite Categories with Your iPhone 11

Homescreen: Hit on the **Health App** icon

Today Summary: Hit on **Summary Tab**

Summary: Hit on **Edit** at the top right angle of the screen page.

Edit Favorite

> ➢ Hit on each desirable Star to add more **Categories.** ★ .
> ➢ As soon as you have completely selected all your preferred **Favorite Categories**, the hit on **Done** at the top right side of the screen.

Hint: When you hit on each star, it will change from frame star ☆ to full blue star ★ .

How You Can Set Up Organ Donation

Homescreen: Hit on the **Health App** icon.

Health: Hit on **Summary Tab**.

Summary: Hit on your **Profile Picture** at the top right side of the page.

Your Name Page: Select **Organ Donor**

Organ Donor: Hit on the **Sign Up with Donate Life** bar to sign up.

Registration

> ➢ All your profile details will display, what you only need is to enter the last four-digit number of your **Social Security Number** (SSN).
> ➢ Hit on the **Continue** button below to complete your registration.

84

- ➢ Hit on **Complete Registration with Donate Life** at the bottom center of the screen.
- ➢ **Thank You:** Hit on the **Done** button below.
- ➢ Your complete registration with Donate Life will show up under your Medical ID profile as **Organ Donor-Donate Life.**

How You Can Solve Health Tracking Steps Failure on Your iPhone 11

For your health tracking steps to be functionally perfect, you need to connect your Apple Watch with your iPhone.

If you are having a challenge of not seeing your steps being tracked by the Health App on your iPhone 11, then take the following steps:

Homescreen: Hit on the **Health App** icon.

Health: Hit on **Summary Tab**.

Summary: Hit on your **Profile Picture** at the top right side of the page.

Your Name Page: Under **Privacy** hit on **Devices**

Devices: Select your **Apple Watch**

Your Watch Privacy: Hit on **Privacy Settings** and activate **Fitness Tracking** by switching On the Activator.

How You Can Set Up Family Sharing

Homescreen: Hit on the **Settings App** icon

Settings: Go to your **Profile Name** at the top

Apple ID: Select Set Up Family Sharing

Family Sharing: Hit on the "**Get Started**" button

Get Started: Select **Location Sharing** or any other feature you want to share. There might be a slightly different method of setup in various other features of family sharing available.

Share Your Location with Your Family: Hit on the **Share Your Location** button at the bottom center of the screen. If you are not ready to share your location you can select the **Not Now** option below.

Invite Your Family: Hit on the **Invite Family Members** bar at the bottom center.

How You Can Track Your Menstrual Cycle with Your iPhone 11

The use of Health apps to track women's menstrual cycle can be fully studied and determined on your iPhone 11 since the iPhone came with iOS 13 which can still be upgraded to iOS 13.5, and you can also use Apple watch running with watchOS 6 to effectively complement your health reading and tracking.

Apple Watch is perfectly used to get an accurate reading of your heartbeat, rate, and general health conditions.

How You Can Set Up Every Month Menstrual Cycle on Your iPhone 11

Homescreen: Hit on the **Health App** icon.

Search: Hit on the **Browse** tab at the bottom right of the screen.

Browse:

> ➤ Select **Cycle Tracking** among the **Health Categories**
> ➤ Hit on the "**Get Started**" button.

Cycle Tracking: Hit on **Options**

Options

> ➤ You will scroll down to select **Period Length** and swipe up to select your period duration e.g. 2 days, 3 days, 4 days, 5days, etc. The period length is the number of days you experience menstrual flow. For example, If you see the menstrual flow from Aug 2 to 5 is equal to 4days.
> ➤ Select **Cycle Length** and swipe up to select the appropriate days before the next menstrual cycle e.g. 25 days or 26 days etc.

Hint: If you are having some pre or post symptoms that come with your cycle you may activate all the relevant suggested contents above **Your Cycle Log.** Some of them are:

1. Spotting
2. Basal Body Temperature
3. Cervical Mucus Quality
4. Ovulation Test Result
5. Sexual Activity
6. Symptoms… and others.

How You Can See Your Cycle Timeline

Homescreen: Hit on the **Health App** icon.

Search: Hit on the **Browse** tab at the bottom right of the screen.

Browse: Select **Cycle Tracking** among the **Health Categories**

The Timeline will appear as:

1. **Solid Circles**: Number of days you recorded for your menstrual period.
2. **Purple Dots**: The number of days you recorded for experiencing symptoms
3. **Light Red Circle:** This is your next menstrual period Prediction.
   - ✓ **For You to Hide or Display Predicted Period Days:** Select **Option** and activate the **Period Prediction** switch.
4. **Light Blue Days:** These predict your possible Fertility Window. You should not use it to guide yourself for birth control.
   - ✓ **For You to Hide or Display Infertility Window:** Select **Option** and activate the **Fertility Prediction** switch.

How You Can Know Your Possible Next Menstrual Cycle

Homescreen: Hit on the **Health App** icon.

Search: Hit on the **Browse** tab at the bottom right of the screen.

Browse: Select **Cycle Tracking** among the **Health Categories**

Cycle Tracking

➢ Scroll down to select **Prediction** under **Cycle Log.** This will enable you to know your next menstrual cycle.
  ✓ **If you are unable to see the evaluation:** Select **Show All** before the prediction option.
➢ Scroll down to select **Statistics.** This will enable you to see all your previous menstrual period and predictive cycle length.

On Apple Watch: For You To Determine Date

➢ Launch the **Cycle Track App.**
➢ Scroll down to select **Period Prediction/Last Menstrual Period.**

How You Can Track All Your Cycle Symptoms in Health App

Homescreen: Hit on the **Health App** icon.

Search: Hit on the **Browse** tab at the bottom right of the screen.

Browse: Select **Cycle Tracking** among the **Health Categories**

Cycle Tracking: Hit on **Options** at front of **Cycle Log**

Options: Activate the **Symptoms** activator to access all the possible symptoms before/during/after the menstrual cycle. All the symptoms are listed below:

- ✓ Abdominal Cramp
- ✓ Acne
- ✓ Appetite
- ✓ Bloating
- ✓ Breast Tenderness
- ✓ Constipation
- ✓ Diarrhea
- ✓ Headache
- ✓ Hot Flashes
- ✓ Lower Back Pain
- ✓ Mood Changes
- ✓ Nausea
- ✓ Ovulation Pain
- ✓ Tiredness
- ✓ Sleep Changes

You can tap on any of the symptoms you are experiencing before or during or after the menstrual cycle to log your symptoms with Cycle Tracking.

How You Can Record Menstrual Cycle Symptoms on Your Apple Watch.

On Apple Watch:

- ➢ To launch Apple tray by pressing **Digital Crown**

- ➢ Select the **Cycle Tracking** App icon
- ➢ Hit on **Symptoms**
- ➢ Scroll through the various available symptoms and hit on various symptoms list you regularly experience before or during or after the menstrual cycle.
- ➢ Hit on **Done**

How You Can Set Up Prediction for Period, fertility, and Notification, through Cycle Tracking

How You Can Track All Your Cycle Symptoms in Health App

Homescreen: Hit on the **Health App** icon.

Search: Hit on the **Browse** tab at the bottom right of the screen.

Browse: Select **Cycle Tracking** among the **Health Categories**

Cycle Tracking: Hit on **Options**

Options: Hit on the activator of the below features to turn them "On".

- ➢ Activate **Period Prediction**.
- ➢ Activate the **Period Notification.**
- ➢ Activate the **Fertility Predictions**
- ➢ Activate **Fertility Notifications.**

How You Can Record A Period Flow Level Through Cycle Tracking on Your Apple Watch

On Apple Watch

- ➢ To launch Apple tray, press **Digital Crown**
- ➢ Select the **Cycle Tracking** App icon
- ➢ In the everyday tracker above the Data Summary hit on the **Day.**
- ➢ Below Menstrual Unit hit on **Period** to record your menstrual flow. Select your period flow level by tapping on any of these options below:
    - ✓ Light
    - ✓ Medium

✓ Heavy

➢ Hit on **Done.**

How You Can Further Record Your Sexual Activity In Cycle Tracking

You can use this to track when last or the period you had sex with your spouse.

Option:

➢ Hit on **Sexual Activity**
➢ On the same page hit on **Sexual Activity** and select **Had Sex**.
➢ Select **Not Used** or **Used** to remind you of your sexual protection.

How You Can Record Your Sexual Activity in Cycle Tracking on Your Apple Watch

On Apple Watch

➢ To launch Apple tray, press **Digital Crown**

➢ Select the **Cycle Tracking** App icon
➢ Hit on **Sexual Activity**
➢ If you had sexual intercourse, then hit on **Had Sex**
➢ For protection confirmation, select **Not Used** or **Used**

How You Can Remove All Cycle Tracking in Health App On Your iPhone.

Homescreen: Hit on the **Health App** icon.

Search: Hit on the **Browse** tab at the bottom right of the screen.

Browse: Select **Cycle Tracking** among the **Health Categories**

Cycle Tracking: Scroll down to select **View Cycle Tracking Items**

View Cycle Tracking Items: Hit on every **Category Log** you wanted to remove.

> ➢ Scroll down to the bottom region to hit on **Show All Data.**
> ➢ At the top right angle of the screen hit on **Edit.**
> ➢ Hit on the **Remove icon** beside the data you wanted to remove.
> ➢ Hit on **Delete.**
> ➢ Hit on **Done** at the top right angle of the screen.

How You Can Know the Source of Your Data for Many Sources

Health App always makes use of the same data from different sources like Apple Watch, iPhone, and iPod. If you are using several Apple devices that are connected with iPhone 11, it very important as a user to specifically know which of the Apple device is responsible for the data making.

You can set your iPhone to be the major source that Health App should be used for data generation, instead of using all available Bluetooth devices. This method is called the **Prioritization of Device.**

Homescreen: Hit on the **Health App** to launch the page.

Summary: Hit on the **Browse** icon tab.

Browse: Hit on a **Category** such as **Activity**.

Activity: Select the **Subcategory** such as Steps or Walk & Running or any other one.

Hint: But if you are unable to see the subcategory you are looking for, then you can scroll up to access the Searching tool at the top of

94

the page. Hit the field and enter the **Subcategory** and it will appear.

Steps: Swipe up to select **Data Sources & Access**

Hint: You will see all the Sources that are responsible for the make of the Steps' Data will be enlisted.

How You Can Access All The General Sources For The Health App

Homescreen: Hit on the **Health App** to launch the page.

Summary: Hit on **Profile Picture** at the top right of the page.

Your Profile Name Page: Move down of the page to Privacy and hit on **Apps or Devices.**

You will see all the Sources that enable Health App to generate those Data.

How You Can Assign Sources for Data

This will enable you to prioritize sources for the making of a particular subcategory data in the Health App.

Homescreen: Hit on the **Health App** to launch the page.

Summary: Hit on the **Browse** icon tab.

Browse: Hit on a **Category** such as **Activity**

Activity: Select the **Subcategory**

Subcategory: You will go down the page and select **Data Source & Access.**

Data Source & Access: Hit on **Edit**

➤ Touch and Hold down **Change Order** Button at the front of the Data Source.

➤ You can either **Drag Up** or **Down** the **Data Source** on the lists.

If you do not want a Data Source to generate Data for the Subcategory: Deactivate the **Activation Switch.**

GUIDE SIX

How You Can Get Used to Apps for Communication on Your iPhone 11

The applications (Apps) that have communication features on your iPhone will enable you to pass across information to people that are very essential to you and also receive information from them. The apps will give you access to hear the live voice of your communicator(s) or recording conversations between them.

More so, through the communication app, you can make live text chat with your dearest fellows or colleagues or business partners or family and instantly receive a reply with the use of cellular data or subscription.

Above all, you can make conference audio or video calls with numerous of people. The Apps the have the **Communication Features** are:

1. Call App
2. FaceTime App
3. Message App
4. Mail App
5. Safari App

Everything You Need to Know About Phone App

 The call app is one of the most essential primary cores of using the iPhone for communication. The use of Call App will enable you rich-out to your people of your through their phone numbers.

The people's phone number could be categorized into two places to separate the most important ones from general ones.

The most inevitable people are considered to be your **Favorites** on the iPhone while others belong to the general **Contacts.** You can assign a separate ringing tone to all contacts in **Favorites.**

By default, the Phone App is specifically positioned at the base bar of the Homescreen to ease your call making and receiving.

To save your friend contact in Phone app contacts, you will need the phone number, first and last name, email (if available), and picture (if available). But, it is very advisable to save your friend's email in the contact detail because you may need to reach him/her through your Email massage.

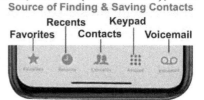

Add Contact

Homescreen: Hit on the **Phone App** at the base bar of your iPhone.

Favorites

> Hit on **Favorite** icon (Star) at the bottom left of the screen.
> Hit on **Add** icon (Cross) at the top left of your iPhone's screen.
> Go through all contact to locate the named contact or enter the name of the person into the **Search field** to quickly see the **Person's Contact.**
> Hit on the Contact Name
> **Optional Dialog Box:** Hit on the usual way of contacting people such as Message (iMessage or Mail), Call, or FaceTime. For example, select Call.
> Immediately, you will see the selected contact name among **Favorites.**

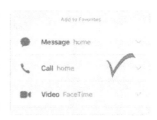

   OR

Homescreen: Hit on the **Phone App** at the base bar of your iPhone.

Contacts

> ➢ Hit on **Contacts Icon** at the bottom center of the iPhone's screen.
> ➢ Hit on the **search field** to quickly locate the contact's name you are looking for.
> ➢ Hit on the contact's name to see all the person's information details, below you will see **Add to Favorites.**
> ➢ Hit on the Contact Name
> **Optional Dialog Box:** Hit on the usual way of contacting people such as Message (iMessage or Mail), Call, or FaceTime. For example, select Call.
> ➢ Immediately, you will see the selected contact name among **Favorites.**

How You Can Remove a Contact from Your iPhone

You need to understand the fact that, whenever you apply to **Delete** command on any contact on your iPhone or Email account, it will completely remove it from your iPhone without a chance of retrieving/restoring it.

Therefore, you have to fully sure about the contact before you hit on **Delete** command.

Homescreen: Hit on **Contacts Icon**

Contacts

> ➢ Search for the **Contact's Name** through the search field
> ➢ Hit on the exact **Contacts Name**
> ➢ Hit on **Edit**
> ➢ Move down the screen to hit on **Delete Contacts.**
> ➢ For confirmation re-tap on **Delete Contacts** (Confirmatory Dialog Box)**. Immediately the contact will be completely removed from your iPhone Contacts' list.

How to Set Organizing Order of Contacts List on Your iPhone

The Names of everyone in your Contacts could be arranged chronological order from A-Z to ease searching of either **First or Second Name.**

You are given the privilege to instruct your iPhone on how you want the name to be arranged, that is if you want the First name to appear before the second the following setting will enable it:

Homescreen: Hit on the **Settings Icon**

Settings: Scroll down to select **Contacts**

Contacts

> ➢ **Sort Order:** This will alphabetically arrange either the First or Second Name in Contacts.
> ➢ **Display Order**: This will either display the First Name after or before Second Name.

Short Name: Select how the Contact's Name of yours will show in Phone, Mail, Messages, FaceTime… and other Apps.

How You Can Successfully Move Contacts from SIM to iPhone

You can transfer all your contacts on your SIM into your new iPhone if the SIM supports the feature it is very easy to do.

SIM Card Insertion: Insert your SIM containing the contacts you want to transfer into your iPhone.

Homescreen: Hit on the **Settings Icon**

Settings: Hit on **Contacts**

Contacts:

> ➢ Move to the middle of the screen to hit on **Import SIM Contacts.**
> ➢ Hit where the contacts should be imported from an optional dialog box that will appear.

➢ Hold on till the whole contacts moving process finished before you proceed.
➢ Access your Contact to confirm the complete importation on iPhone.

Hints: iPhone cannot save the contact(s) on SIM card, if you want to transfer contacts from iPhone to iPhone then there will be a need for you to back-up the iPhone with iCloud storage or other transferring means like PC memory, flash, etc.

How You Can Activate and Deactivate Contacts for Mail Account

The activation of Contacts will enable you to add contacts in any of your Email Account and deactivation of Contacts will enable the removal of contact(s) from your iPhone.

Homescreen: Hit **Settings Icon**

Settings: Hit on **Password and Account**

Password and Account: Hit on the **Email Account.**

The Email Account (Gmail/Yahoo): Switch On the **Contacts Activator** to become Green.

To Deactivate Contacts App

The Email Account (Gmail/Yahoo)

➢ Switch Off the **Contacts Activator** to become **White.**
➢ Hit **Delete from My iPhone.** Immediately the contact will be removed.

How You Can Set a Particular Email Account for Your Contacts

Homescreen: Hit **Settings Icon**

Settings: Hit on **Password and Account**

Password and Account: Hit on **Add Account**

Add Account: Hit on your Email account and switch On **Contacts.**

If you do not have an email account you can hit on **Other** to make Contact Account such as LDAP or CardDAV account is available.

> ➢ Type your details and password.
> ➢ Hit on **Next.**

In a situation whereby you are having several accounts set up in the Contacts App and you need a particular account for the contacts:

Homescreen: Hit on **Contacts** App

Contacts: Hit **Groups** at the top left angle of the screen.

How You Can Add a New Contact to Your Default Account

This is very advisable for you if you are using more than one Email Account in your **Contacts.**

Homescreen: Hit on **Settings Icon**

Settings: Scroll down to select **Contacts**

Contacts: Hit on **Default Account**

Default Account: Select **One** of your **Email Accounts.**

How You Can Make Perfect Call

Homescreen: Hit on **Phone App**

Keypad Interface

> ➢ Type the **Contact Number** if you do not have the person's contact in your iPhone **Contact List.**
> ➢ Hit on the **Call Button.** It is the Green

Circle.

End Call

- ➢ The Green Circle Button will change to Red Circle Button, it is called the **End Button.**
- ➢ Hit the **End Button** to stop the call.

Make A Call from Contacts

Keypad Interface: Look at the bottom center to hit on **Contacts.**

Contacts:

- ➢ Enter the first-two alphabetical letter that started the name of the person into the search field to speed up the quick discovery of the contact.
- ➢ Hit on the **Contact's Name**

Contact's Name: Hit on the person's Phone Number.

End Call: Hit the **End Button** to stop the call.

How You Can Add People's Phone Number to Your Contact Directly

Keypad Interface

- ➢ Dial the **Phone Number** of the person correctly.
- ➢ Hit on **Add to Contact** at the top of the screen.

Request Dialog Box: On a displayed **Request Dialog Box** hit **Create New Contact.**

Create New Contact

- ➢ Type the First and Second Names

- ➤ Enter the Email of the owner of the Phone Number if you know it (optional).
- ➤ You can choose different **Ringtones** for the contact it is optional.
- ➤ Hit on **Add to Existing Contact**

Add to Existing Contact

- ➤ Look for the **Contact**
- ➤ Enter the Number into the Number text field
- ➤ Hit on **Done.**

Add To Contacts from Recent Called or Received Contacts

You can add the recently ended call phone number into your general Contact by following these steps on your iPhone.

Keypad Interface: Look below and hit **Recents** with a round clock icon.

Recent

- ➤ You will see the recently ended phone number
- ➤ Hit on the **Info icon** in front of the phone number.

Info: Select **Create New Contact**

Create New Contact

- ➤ Type the First and Second Names
- ➤ Enter the Email of the owner of the Phone Number if you know it (optional).
- ➤ You can choose different **Ringtones** for the contact it is optional.
- ➤ Hit on **Add to Existing Contact**

Add to Existing Contact

- ➤ Look for the **Contact**
- ➤ Enter the Number into the Number text field

➢ Hit on **Done.**

Now the recent call will appear with the name you used in the adding of the number into your Contacts. The person contact can be found in your overall **Contacts list** on your iPhone.

How to Delete all Recent Contacts

A recent list comprises of the phone numbers of all those you have called, received calls and missed incoming calls, and missed outgoing calls with day and time they were called or received. You can easily remove all the recent history.

Homescreen: Hit on **Phone App Icon**

Keypad Interface: look at the bottom left of the screen and hit on **Recents** (Round Clock Icon).

Recents

➢ Look at the top left of the screen hit on **Clear**
➢ Hit on the **Clear All Recents** button showing down the screen. If you hit the **Cancel** button, it will reverse the action and the recent list will not be deleted.

How You Can Get Special Ringtones for Calls, Messages, Alert, & Mail

Different ringtones could be fixed to various contacts on your iPhone Contacts. The same ringtone could be given to some particular contacts and separate ringtones could be given to separate contacts in Favorites with vibration to quickly recognize all the important calls on your iPhone.

You can use ringtone to know when closed family members in the Favorites are calling and when your important business partners are also calling.

Homescreen: Hit on **Settings**

Settings: Hit on **Sound & Hepatics**

Sound & Hepatics

> ➢ Hit on the **Vibrate on Ring** activator to turn Green
> ➢ Hit on the **Vibrate on Silence** activator to turn Green
> ➢ Select your **Ringtone** and choose any of the default Ringtones available.

Specific Ringtone for Individual Contact

Homescreen: Hit on **Contact App** icon

Contacts

> ➢ Search for contact through the search field.
> ➢ Hit on the **Contact**
> ➢ Hit on **Edit**
> ➢ Hit on **Ringtone**
> ➢ Select one of the **Default Ringtones**.
> ➢ Make **Home Swipe Up**.

What You Can Do When You Are on a Call

1. You can switch it to outside **Speaker**
2. You can switch to Video Call.
3. You can allow more people to your discussion.
4. You Mute the Voice.
5. You can Accept or Decline other incoming calls.
6. You can compose a message to reply to your call.
7. You can make use of Remind Me to program a remainder to later return the call of the caller.
8. You can search through apps (e.g. Mail, Photo, Note, Calendar, Safari, Social Media) to get relevant information. Browsing Apps will require a Wi-Fi network connection on your iPhone.

How to Allow or Prevent Call When You Are On A Call

To Accept Call: On the calling, the interface slides the Call button toward the right to answer the call.

To Prevent the Call and Forward It into Voicemail: Double-click the **Switch Button** at the right side of the iPhone.

Send Message To Caller: Hit on **Message Icon** to text messages and send them to your caller.

Use Reminder To Recall: You can hit on **Remind Me** to instruct reminding me to call the caller after you stop the current call.

Recalling of Forwarded Calls from Voicemail

Voicemail has a feature that can play your recorded voice greeting to tell the reason why you are not available to receive calls at the moment and also record and play the voice of the caller that audibly delivered messages for a very short time for you to hear.

You can also choose a greeting out of some default recorded greetings for your outgoing greeting.

To make Voicemail to be active you have to go into the Setting or through Voicemail Icon in the Phone app to Set Up your **Password and Greeting**.

Homescreen: Hit on the **Phone App** icon.

Keypad Interface: below the screen hit on **Voicemail Icon** at the last bottom left.

Voicemail: Hit on **Set Up Now.**

Password

> ➤ Type in the **Voicemail Password** that must be in 4-digit.
> ➤ Retype the same **Voicemail Password** to confirm your consistency.

Greeting

> Hit on **Custom** options to make your outgoing greeting with your voice or otherwise.
> Hit on **Record** to start. (Say your greeting as you want it to be said).
> Hit on **Stop** to end the recording.
> Hit on **Play** to hear your recorded greeting.
> If you are not okay, you can re-tap the **Record.**
> If you are okay then hit on **Save**

How to Reset Voicemail Set Up Through Settings

Homescreen: Hit on the **Settings icon.**

Settings: Select **Phone App**

Phone: Hit on **Change Voicemail Password**

Password

> Hit on **New Password**
> Type in the **Previous Password**
> Type in the **New Password**
>> Hit on **Done.**

 ## How to Listening to Your Voicemail

If you are having calls that have been forwarded into Voicemail, you will see the notification number of new Voicemails at the top-right edge side of the **Voicemail Icon** at the last bottom left of the keypad interface.

Homescreen: Hit on the **Phone App** icon.

Keypad Interface: below the screen hit on **Voicemail Icon** at the last bottom left.

Voicemail

> Hit on **Message**

> Hit on **Play** to hear the recorded caller's voice.

➢ Hit on **Call Back** to replay the voice message.
➢ If you are satisfied with the message you can hit on Delete.

To Call the Voicemail

Homescreen: Hit on the **Phone App** icon.

Keypad Interface: below the screen hit on **Voicemail Icon** at the last bottom left.

Voicemail:

➢ Hit on **Call Voicemail.**
➢ Hit on **End Button.**

Send Junk and Unwanted Callers into Voicemail

This is will only allow the saved contacts on your iPhone to ring-out but unknown contacts will be sent to Voicemail

Homescreen: Hit on the **Settings icon.**

Settings: Tap on **Phone**

Phone: Hit on the **Salience Unknown Caller** activator to become Green.

Set Call Waiting in Settings

Wi-Fi Network connection is very important to make Wi-Fi call active in Dual SIM. You will see Call Waiting when one line call is active and another incoming call occurs in another line.

Homescreen: Hit on **Settings**

Settings: Hit on **Phone App**

Phone: Select **Call Waiting** and hit on the activator to become Green.

➢ Make Home Swipe Up

GUIDE SEVEN

The Complete Benefits of FaceTime App on Your iPhone 11

FaceTime App can majorly be used to boost relationships through video, audio, and message communication with others on your iPhone Contacts.

It has a unique video communication feature that can enable you to see the face of the person you are calling or the person that called you.

Most of the time, it is important that you first and foremost send a request to the person you want to make a FaceTime video call with on either interactive iMessages interface or through an audio call that you will like to make or switch to FaceTime Video Call.

You have to ensure that the persons are using the iPhone and you are having enough Wi-Fi Data to make the call.

You can also use FaceTime to make Conference Video Call with other iPhone users in your contacts but you must notify those that will participate in the conference call on text message interface the time, the reason for the group discussion, and ask each of them if they will be available.

Make FaceTime Set Up in Settings to be Active

Homescreen: Hit on **Settings Icon**

Settings: Scroll down to select **FaceTime**

FaceTime

- ➢ Put On the **FaceTime** Activator to become Green
- ➢ Put On the **FaceTime Live Photo** Activator to become Green
- ➢ Provide your **Phone Number**

110

➤ Provide your **Apple ID**

➤ Provide your **Email Add** (Optional)

Make FaceTime Audio Calls or Video Call

Homescreen: Hit on **FaceTime Icon**

FaceTime: Hit on **Add Contact** at the top right of the screen.

Contact: Use the search field to quickly get the contact.

Audio Call: Hit on the **Audio Call button** to fix the audio call.

OR

Video Call: Hit on the **Video Call button** to fix the video call.

How to Change from Normal Audio Calls to FaceTime Video Call

On the calling interface, you will see an option of using FaceTime Video

Video Call: Hit on the **Video Call button** to fix a video call.

Hit on the **End button** at the lower left of the FaceTime Video call interface.

How You Can Change from Text Message Interaction to FaceTime Call

Homescreen: Hit on **Messages App Icon**

Message

> Hit on the **Compose icon** at the top right of the screen.

> Type the name of the person you want to chat with into the **"To"** Search field.
> During the live iMessage chatting with your friend, hit on the name of your friend at the top center of the screen to choose FaceTime.
> Hit on **FaceTime Icon**
> Choose either **Audio or Video Call**
> Hit on the End button to end the FaceTime call

How You Can Make Multiple Chat

Homescreen: Hit on **Messages App Icon**

Messages

> Hit on the **Compose icon** at the top right of the screen.

> Type the **Names or Phone Number or Email Add** of all persons you want to chat with into the **"To"** Search field. For example, *Hannah Berm, Daniel Rose, Dan Floral*
> Below the screen hit the text message field for **Keyboard** to show-up, type your text message, and hit on the **Send**

icon to deliver your message into the chat interface. ⬆

How You Can Change from the Group Conversation to FaceTime Video Call

It is the same step of moving from a single chat that you will take to change your discussion to FaceTime Video or Audio Call.

Message (Chatting Page)

> Hit on the names of your friends at the top center of the screen to choose **FaceTime**.
> Hit on **FaceTime Icon**
> Choose either **Audio or Video Call**
> Hit on the **End button** to end the FaceTime call

How You Can Replace Your Face with Animoji during FaceTime Video

Homescreen: Launch **FaceTime** App

FaceTime

- ➤ On the FaceTime Call interface hit on the **Video Call button.**
- ➤ Hit on **Effect Button.**
- ➤ Hit on either **Memoji** or **Animoji** available
- ➤ Scroll toward the right or left to choose.
- ➤ Hit on your preferred Memoji or Animoji. Immediately your face will be replaced with the chosen Memoji or Animoji.
- ➤ To remove the Memoji or Animoji hit on **Cancel** and your face reappear normally.

If you want to change the current Memoji or Animoji: Restart all over from the beginning of the above process and reselect the new Memoji of Animoji of your choice.

Other Beneficial Things You Can Get In Message App

You can majorly use Messages App to make a direct live chat with those who are in your iPhone contacts using iPhone through iMessage.

Also, you can use it to send a text message to those who are in your contacts using Android.

How to Compose and Reply Text Messages

Homescreen: Hit on **Messages App Icon**

Messages

- ➤ Hit on the **Compose icon** at the upper right of the screen.

113

- ➤ Type the name of the person you want to chat with into the "**To**" Search field.
  OR
- ➤ If you want to reply to any received message in the massage App, hit on the particular message. It will launch you into the compose text message interface.
- ➤ Hit the text field to type your text message.
- ➤ Hit the **Send Button,** that is, the Blue Send Button is for iMessage ⬆ while Green Send Button is for SMS ⬆.

Your iPhone will automatically determine if the text message is iMessage or SMS. Once you see the blue button showing for sending your text message that implies you are about to send iMessage to the person using iPhone but if it shows green that means, you are sending text SMS to an Android user.

How to add Emoji to your Text Message

Messages

- ➤ At the lower left side of the Keyboard hit on **Emoji** Icon
- ➤ You may scroll up and down or right side to select by tapping on anyone you like.
- ➤ Hit on the Send button to move it into the chat interface.

How You Can Add Effects to Your Text Message

Messages

- ➤ At the immediate left side of the Keyboard Text Field, you will see **App Store** Icon, hit on it
- ➤ Select the **Animoji icon** at the bottom roll menu 😮 .
- ➤ You will see different **Animoji** images.
- ➤ Select Animoji you like and position it within the square view guide. Once the Animoji is registered, it will be mimicking your face and mouth movement.

114

- ➤ Hit on **Recording Button** at the lower right side of the view frame to start recording your audio voice with Animoji. ■
- ➤ Hit on the same button to stop the recording and change the button to the **Send** button. It will replay itself for you to hear.
- ➤ If you are satisfied then hit on the **Send button** to forward the Animoji into the **Chat** interface for the person you are chatting with to receive and access.
- ➤ You can still reselect another Animoji below by scrolling through the arranged Animoji drawer and hit on another different Animoji to make a new recording.
- ➤ If you are not satisfied hit on the **Delete** button at the upper right. 🗑

For Additional Effects

- ➤ You can still go-ahead to get more Animoji in the App Store by tapping on the **App Store** icon at the lower-left corner of the screen and hit on **View Apps.**
- ➤ You can still search for "**Images**" that are very accurate to your message by tapping on the **Search Icon** below. 🔍
- ➤ Hit on Find Images Field showing above the displayed images.
- ➤ Enter the types of images you are looking for like Thinking, Disagreement, Excitement, Sleeping, Busy, Hungry, Disturbed, Listening, Working… and many others. You may pick from the appearing keywords as you are entering the word.
- ➤ There is also a **Free Hand Drawing icon** that could allow you to draw anything you like and send it to the person you are chatting with. ⚫
- ➤ You can also send home videos through **YouTube, Audio Music, Recents Selfie Pictures/other Pictures, or Video** through Camera.

How You Can Make Your Own Animoji or Memoji on Your iPhone 11

➢ At the immediate left side of the Keyboard Text Field, you will see **App Store** Icon, hit on it.

➢ Select the **Animoji icon** at the bottom roll menu 🐵 .

➢ Scroll toward right hit on Add/Cross Sign for **New Memoji**

➢ Select **Skin** and adjust it with the available set of colors and remove face spots by choosing freckles.

➢ Select **Hairstyle** to choose either male hairstyle or female hairstyle

➢ Move to **Head Shape** to select the loveliest chin.

➢ Move to the **Eye** section to pick the type of eye you like having on your Memoji.

➢ Continue to select all the parts of the face of your Memoji from the other options including **Browse, Nose & Lips, Ear** with different pretty earing, **Facial Hair** with either Mustard & Beard or Sideburns, **Eyewear** like glasses, and **Headwear** like face-caps, hat, etc., till you complete achieve a beautiful looking Memoji. It is a creative place that is full of fun.

➢ As soon as you are satisfied with your **Self Making Memoji** then hit on **Done** to save the Memoji and include it with the group of Animoji.

You can use your Memoji to make FaceTime video call or iMessage audio chat on the Message App interface of your iPhone.

How to Add Animation Effect to Your Key Text Message

➢ Type your short text message into the text field. For example, *Stay Home Safe, Drink Responsibly, Daily Exercise Importance, Let's Jubilate, Today's Plan, etc.*

➢ Press down the **Send** button for a while to launch **Effect Page** contains:

- ✓ **Bubble Animation Effects:** Slam, Loud, Gentle and Invisible Ink.
- ✓ **Screen Animation Effects:** Send with Echo, Send with Confetti, Send with Spotlight… and ⊗ others.

Send with Effect

- ➤ At the upper center of the page, you will see **Bubble & Screen.**
- ➤ Hit one of the various effects menu to know the best. Once you have known the best leave it on the option.
- ➤ Hit on the **Screen** option above.
- ➤ Swipe the screen from right to left to see the various screen effects. When you have seen the most suitable **Screen Effect** for your Text message then hit on the **Send** button.
- ➤ If you are not satisfied then hit on the **Cancel** button to return to the message interface.

How to Send Voice Message

This makes the message easy for those who are not having enough time to chat or who are not very fast in a typing text message to quickly deliver their messages, as a result, they choose a short audio recording message that is précised, specific, and facts.

Messages

- ➤ Go to the bottom left of the keyboard and hit on **Microphone Icon.**
- ➤ Start an audio message. You will see the linear sound wave of your voice as you are talking. The louder your voice the larger the width of the sound wave.
- ➤ As soon as you finished the audio message the hit **Send** button above.
- ➤ It will be seen in the chat interface.
- ➤ Look at the bottom left of the screen and hit on the Keyboard icon to return the Keyboard.

Hint: You can also dictate your message to Siri that is capable of changing all your audio dictation messages to text messages and sent it to the right contact you commanded.

More of What You Can Do With Mail App

 Mail app is an avenue to receive and send a message(s) with the use of Electronic Mail (Email) Service Providers which include **Google** (...@gmail.com), **Yahoo** (...@ yahoo.com), **iCloud** (...@icloud.com), **Outlook.com** (...@outlook.com)... and many others.

The use of the Mail App will fully allow you to receive or send documents to loved ones and business associates. It is more officially use for a better transaction between you and other business organizations.

Mail has become the most reliable acceptable official interactive platform to provide your vital details and execution of online obligation.

Therefore, the essential processes for you to become a wonderful beneficiary user of Mail great opportunities.

There are channels through which you can get information from that can be added to your composed message such addition is called **Document Attachment.**

You can save documents with any **Microsoft Office** formats or you may directly go to a website to copy very relevant information that is helpful to clarify your message and subsequently paste it within your message.

If you already have two or more email accounts and you want to add them to your new iPhone there are some simple steps you have to do in your iPhone Settings.

To make Mail effectively functional, then you have to carry-out either manual or automatic setup in Settings on your iPhone.

How You Can Effectively Enable Mail App Set Up Manually

The manual is simply designed for those who are using different Emails from the suggested email accounts on the Add Account Interface. Then, the **Other** is the correct option to choose.

Homescreen: Hit on the **Settings** icon.

Settings: Move down and select **Accounts & Passwords.**

Accounts & Passwords: Hit on **Add Account**

Add Account: Look at the lower region of the screen and hit on **Other.**

Other: Hit on **Add Mail Account**

New Account

> ➤ Type your **Name**
> ➤ Type your specific **Email Account**
> ➤ Type your **Password**
> ➤ Type your **Description**
> ➤ Hit on **Next** for the setup to be finalized and the Mail will search for your Email Account.
> ➤ Once the searching is successful then hit on **Done.**

If the Email Account Settings could not be found by Mail then do the following to roundup the setup.

Second Phase New Account: If you do not know your Email settings ask your email service provider to tell you if the email settings belong to IMAP or POP. As soon as, you confirm

➢ Hit on **IMAP/POP**
➢ Provide details on **INCOMING & OUTCOMING MAIL SERVER**
    ✓ **Host Name**
    ✓ **User Name & Password**
➢ Hit on **Next** at the top.
➢ Once your details are accurate then hit in **Save**

Your inability to provide the correct details will lead to the inability to complete the manual setup.

How You Can Effectively Enable Mail App Set Up Automatically

Homescreen: Hit on the **Settings** icon.

Settings: Move down and select **Accounts & Passwords.**

Accounts & Passwords: Hit on **Add Account**

Add Account: Select your Email service source (e.g. Yahoo).

Yahoo

➢ Type your existing **Yahoo Address**
➢ Type correct **Password**

(If you want to look into your email account then you can hit on **Sign In**, when you are through, then **Sign Out** to return to the previous Set Up page because you still have some tasks to complete. Better still, complete the tasks before you Sign-In into your account).

120

➤ Hit on **Next** to continue and hold on for the processing to complete.

➤ Switch On the **Activator** of the following applications **Contacts App, Mail Contacts, Calendar App, Note App & Reminder App.**
➤ At the top right region of the screen hit on **Save.**

How to Activate the Function of Essential Tools for Message Composition

All essential tools for a perfect write up and excellent message composition should be activated in the Settings to ensure correct spellings, arrangement, capitalization… and many others.

Homescreen: Hit on the **Settings icon**

Settings: Select **General**

General: Select **Keyboards**

Keyboards: Switch On the following **Activation buttons** of **Auto-Capitalization, Auto-Correction, Check Spelling, Enable Caps Lock, Predictive, Smart Punctuation, Character Preview, Shortcut, and Enable Dictation.**

To Change Your Keyboard to One-Handed Keyboard

On the same Keyboards page

Keyboards: Select **One-Handed Keyboard** and hit on the **Activator**

OR

You can also get the selection of One-Handed Keyboard directly on the Mail to compose page.

Homescreen: Hit on **Mail App**

Mail: Hit the **Compose icon** at the top right region of the screen or select received Email and later hit on compose or reply icon.

New Message

> ➤ Hit the front of "**To:**" for text cursor to show and the Keyboard to show below.
> ➤ At the lower region of the Keyboard in the new message interface, press down the Earth icon for different types of Keyboard to show.
> ➤ Hit on either left or right-hand side Keyboard that is very convenient for you.

How to Write and Send Email Messages

Homescreen: First and foremost, go to the **Control Center** to put On Wi-Fi Network and hit on **Mail App**

Mail: Hit Compose Icon at the top right region of the screen or select received Email and later hit on compose or reply icon.

New Message

> ➤ Hit the front of "**To:**" for the text cursor to show and the Keyboard to show below.
> ➤ Type the **Name or Email Address** of the receiving contact (the person's or company's email address).
> ➤ Hit the front of "**Subject:**" to type a short theme of your message.
> ➤ Hit on the text field interface to start writing your text message. Once you are through then hit on the **Send icon** at the top right region of the screen.
> ➤ How to Directly Get Name or Email from Your iPhone Contact

You can directly get the name or email address of the person you want to send an email message to through the Contacts on your iPhone.

New Message: Hit on the **Add/Cross** icon to launch Contacts and use the search field to quickly locate the contact you are looking for.

How to Attach Document to Your Message

It is advisable to attach a PDF or JPEG document to your Email because the document cannot be altered.

Mail: Hit Compose Icon at the top right region of the screen or

select received Email and later hit on compose or reply icon.

New Message: After you have entered the above "**To**" info (name or email add of where you are sending a message)**, Subject and** You have composed your message.

- ➤ Press down anywhere on the message field for **Edit Menu** to show.
- ➤ Hit on the **Arrow** at the end of the **Edit menu** to select **Add Attachment.**
- ➤ It will open to your iPhone document storage and iCloud Drive. Navigate through the App you used such as **Pages App, Keynotes App...** and others.

For Photo or Video

- ➤ You can also attach pictures to your message by tapping or press down the field and be tapping on the arrow at the end till you will see **Insert Photo** or **Video.**
    - ✓ It will launch out your Photo library to select your **Pictures.** Carefully navigate through the exact category you have your pictures.
    - ✓ Hit on your **Pictures** and **Send** them to upload on your massage field.

Copy Information from Website

✓ At the down middle of the iPhone Notch slide-down a little to see the App browsing text field.
✓ Enter Safari, you will see the App and hit on it to access the web page.
✓ Enter web add, highlight the massage, and hit copy.
✓ Go to the base of the horizontal bar and swipe from the left end to the right end. You will see the New Message page.
✓ Hit the place you want to paste the copied info to display on the message field for the edit menu to show an option of **Paste.** Hit Paste and what you copied will display.

OR

Homescreen: Hit on Safari to launch the web add text field.
✓ Copy your message as explained above.
✓ Move your finger from the middle bottom of the iPhone in inverted seven Γ to see the minimized **New Message Page**. (go to **Guide Four** learn "How to see reduced app pages")
✓ Hit on the New Message Page and follow the above pasting steps.
➤ Once you are through with all the documents attachment, then hit on **Send** ⬆.

All You Can Ask Siri To Do For You Through Voice Dictation

Siri features will help you to organize and properly program your daily, weekly, monthly, and yearly activities successfully.

It is a unique tool iPhone that can help you to operate all the applications on your iPhone quickly and easily. Siri can help you activate any app or control on your iPhone.

Siri can supply you with all current information happening around the world; it could tell you the climatic condition as the moment, traffic condition, reminding you of every important saved event in your organizer or calendar.

Siri could help you set an alarm when you ask it to do so. It can change your dictated message to a text message and send it to the instructed contact. It can translate the English language to any other language like French, German, Spanish... and more others.

It can help you locate a place on a Google map and show you the bearing compass to get the place. It can assist you to find out a review or reputation about an organization or person.

Siri can tell you where you can locate your favorites using iPhone that you have already registered with Siri. It could help you forward calls to your acquainted favorites or anyone in your contact... many other benefits.

When you call Siri, you will hear a human voice that could be a female or male voice. It depends on the types of sex voice you choose during Siri Setup.

However, for you to know all that Siri could do on your iPhone for you.

What to Do First with Siri

For Siri to work on your iPhone you must first and foremost finish the setup in the settings, if you have not done it during the iPhone Automatic Setup or Manual Setup.

Homescreen: Hit on **Settings**

Settings: Move down to select **Siri & Search**

Siri & Search: Put On all the below **Activation Buttons** and select your preferable features for each option.

> ➢ Listen for "Hey Siri".
> ➢ Press Side Button for Siri.

- ➢ Allow Siri When Locked.
- ➢ Language.
- ➢ Siri Voice.
- ➢ Voice Feedback.
- ➢ My Information.
- ➢ **SIRI SUGGESTIONS**
  - ✓ Suggestion in Search
  - ✓ Suggestions in Lock Up

Lock Screen or Homescreen:

- ➢ Unlock the iPhone (If you did not activate " When Locked")
- ➢ Press the Switch, Sleep, or Wake Button on the right side of your iPhone. (If you have activated "Press Side Button for Siri")
- ➢ **Say**: Hey Siri! What can Siri do
- ➢ Siri will respond and show you all things that it could do.

You can also use Apple Earpods to call the attention of Siri

- ➢ Click the Answering middle button to call Siri's attention.

Without Clicking on Side Button on Homescreen

- ➢ Say: Hey Siri!
- ➢ Immediately Siri will answer you. Siri is very sensitive to "Hey Siri", and then continue with your question.

How You Can Fully Use Safari App on Your iPhone

 Safari App on your iPhone makes use of Cellular Service and Wi-Fi Network Data to facilitate the efficiency, however, without network and data you cannot access Safari App.

The use of the Safari app will give the privilege of visiting many websites and move from a webpage to another webpage to gather several details or facts online.

Safari suggests a more related website that you can get more useful messages and also display all the favorite websites.

You can download or save apps through the Safari browser on your iPhone into My iPhone or iCloud drive. The Safari browsing window is loaded with many beneficial tools like:

- ➤ **Page Icon:** To move from webpage to another webpage ⬜
  - ✓ **Add New Tab (Add Icon ╬)** to add more **Tab**
  - ✓ **Private** to open a confidential browsing window.
  - ✓ **Close Icon** to delete the page at the top left edge ✕
  - ✓ **Done**
- ➤ **Share Icon** to send a page to other apps like Mail, Message, Add to Notes, Bookmark, Reading List, etc.; or to social media page which will be displayed the options of where you can save the webpage. Check any of the below options to determine what format the document will be sent:
  - ✓ **Automatic:** It will select the exact appropriate format for every application or action
  - ✓ **PDF**
  - ✓ **Web Archive**
- ➤ **Download Icon** to access the recent download files on Safari. ⊕
- ➤ **URL with A Small and A Big (AA):** Small A is used to reduce the font size and the big A is to increase the font size. It is designed to enable the following settings:
  - ✓ Small A Font Size Settings
  - ✓ Big A Size Settings
  - ✓ Show Reader View ▤
  - ✓ Hide Toolbar ↘
  - ✓ Request Desktop Website 🖥
  - ✓ Website Settings ⊘

How to Put the Safari Settings in Place

Homepage: Hit on **Settings**.

Settings: Scroll down the screen and hit on **Safari**

Safari

> ➤ **SEARCH**
> Allow Safari to access Siri by tapping on **Siri & Search** and Activate the switch.
> ➤ **SEARCH**
> > ✓ **Search Engine** will select your preferable source e.g. Google.
> > ✓ Put On the **Searching Engine Suggestions** Activator.
> > ✓ Put On the **Safari Suggestions** Activator.
> > ✓ Hit on **Quick Website Search** to select **On**
> > ✓ Put On the **Preload Top Hit** Activator.
> ➤ **GENERAL**
> > ✓ Activate **Autofill**
> > ✓ Put On the **Frequency Visited Sites** Activator.
> > ✓ Put On the **Favorite** Activator
> > ✓ Hit on **Favorites** to select **Favorites**
> > ✓ Put On the **Block Pop-up** Activator
> > ✓ Put On the **Show Link Previews** Activator
> > ✓ Hit on **Download** to select the storage source e.g. My iPhone and iCloud.
> ➤ **TABS**
> > ✓ Put On **Show Tab Bar** Activator
> > ✓ If you want Icons to be shown in the Tab then you may put On **Show Icons in Tabs'** activation button.
> > ✓ Hit on **Open Links** to select **In New Tab**
> > ✓ Hit on **Close Tabs** to select when you want the open tabs to be closed automatically by Safari. (e.g. Manually, After One Day, After One Week or After One Month).
> ➤ **PRIVACY & SECURITY**
> > ✓ Put On **Prevent Cross-Site Tracking** activator.
> > ✓ Do not activate **Block All Cookies** because they cannot transmit viruses and your iPhone details cannot be hacked by the network hackers.
> > ✓ Put On **Fraudulent Websites Warning's** activator

✓ Put On **Check for Apple Pay** activator: it will enable you to if the Apple Pay activated and if you are having an Apple Account.
➢ **Clear History and Website Data:** If you hit this option you will be able to clear all the browsing history and website data on your iPhone.
➢ **SETTING FOR WEBSITE**
  ✓ Hit on **Page Zoom** for selection between 50%-300% but you may choose 100% for the normal setting.
  ✓ Hit on **Request Desktop Website** for a selection of Websites.
  ✓ Hit on **Reader** for selection
  ✓ Hit on **Camera** for selection of Image Size.
  ✓ Hit on **Microphone** for selection
➢ **READING LIST**
  ✓ You can activate **Automatically Save Offline** if you want all reading lists in the iCloud to be automatically saved.
  ✓ Hit on **Advance** for selection.

How You Can Efficiently Start Safari Browsing on Your iPhone

Homescreen: Hit on **Safari Icon** at the lower bar menu of the page.

Safari:

➢ Hit on the **Browsing Text Field** to type in your searching words from the appeared keyboard.
  ✓ You may select from the predictive dropdown keywords.
  ✓ You may also type your web address directly if you are very sure about it.
➢ Hit on the "**Go**" button on your keyboard and what you are looking for will come up.
  If you are searching for social media applications like Facebook, WhatsApp... and many others then hit on the

app or hit on the download option if you want to download on your iPhone.

For **Webpage**: Once the page is displayed "you want to save the page as **Bookmark** for future or reference purpose".

✓ Hit on **Bookmark Icon** at the bottom of the page.

✓ Select **Add Bookmark for 3 Tabs** on the informative dialog box to **Save** it inside a **New Folder.**

✓ **New Folder:** Give the **Web Tab** a Name, hit on **Done** and it will be saved in the Favorite browsing tabs.

✓ If you want to open the web tab later. Hit on Bookmark and select the Name of the web tab and the page will open.

➢ **About Favorites:** These are the websites you visit often and automatically displayed below your Safari browsing search field.

✓ You can just hit on any of the come web icons to directly launch the webpage of the website without you retyping the website address into the search field machine.

✓ It is very easy and pretty cool to use.

✓ If still want to open another website, all you need to do is to hit on **Add New Tab** Icon at the right bottom of the screen.

✓ A new page with your favorite websites will be displayed then hit on the other website to also launch another webpage for you to access easily.

➢ **Move From Tab Page To Tab Page**

✓ Hit on the Switch Page Icon at the last right bottom of the screen.

✓ You will see all the open pages filed up behind one another. With the help of your finger slightly swipe down to reselect any of the pages by tapping on the page.

- ✓ **Delete Tab Page:** Look at the top left edge of each page you will see **Cancel Icon**, tap on it and the tab page will be deleted.

➢ **Other Places You Can Save Your Place**

- ✓ Hit on the **Share Icon** to access the various apps that you can choose and save the web tap, as mentioned above.

➢ **Use Share Icon to Transfer Webpage from Your iPhone to Another Apple Device**

- ✓ Go to the bottom of the page and hit on the **Share icon.**
- ✓ Select on **AirDrop** Icon
- ✓ Locate the Apple device **Name** and select. On the other Apple device hit **Accept** on the informative dialog box; instantly you will see the **Webpage** on the other Apple device screen.

What You Can Do When Webpage Is Not Loading on Safari or Safari Not Responding

There are major technical problems that could prevent Safari from not responding or failed to load the webpage.

1. **Wi-Fi Network:** First and foremost ensure that there is an effective network of the Wi-Fi connection on your iPhone.
   - ✓ **Problem 1:** If your Wi-Fi network is perfectly connected and there is no visible network indication on your iPhone.
   - ✓ **Solution 1:** Relocate yourself to a place where you can see the Wi-Fi network because the stronger the Wi-Fi network the more Safari will be efficiently responding to the loading webpage.

How to Reactivate the Wi-Fi Network in Setting

Homescreen: Hit on **Settings Icon**

Settings: Select **Wi-Fi**

Wi-Fi: Put Off the **Wi-Fi** Activator 40secs and re-put it On. Go back to Settings and select **Mobile Data.**

Mobile Data: Put Off the **Mobile Data** Activator for a 40secs and re-put it On. Go back to Settings and select **General**

General: Select **Reset**

Reset

- ➢ Select **Reset Network Settings**
- ➢ Hit on the **Enter Password** that will show below.

Enter Password: Type in the **Password** and confirm the **Safari.**

Second Possible Problem

- ✓ **Problem 2:** If you are having s strong Wi-Fi network and Safari is not responding or loading a webpage.
- ✓ **Solution 2:** Crosscheck the Safari settings as some had been stated above and while the rest will be discussed below under **Settings.**
2. **Settings Crosschecking:** Initially go through all the Safari Settings above. Move a little further by tapping on **Advanced** to confirm the various activations of Safari Settings.

Homescreen: Hit on **Settings Icon**

Settings: Scroll down to select **Safari**

Safari: Start verifying the activated buttons one by one till you get to **Advanced**. Hit on the **Advanced.**

Advanced: Hit on each activation button to put Off and put On again. If you have not activated the below features on your iPhone before ensure that you activate them all because they are very important.

- ✓ **Advanced:** Initially turn Off the feature one by one to confirm the Safari response, if it is working fine. But, if it is not yet responding put On the feature

132

and repeat the same action on the next feature till you get the one that is responsible for the Safari abnormality.

- Re-put On the **JavaScript** activation button.
- Select **Experimental Features.**

✓ **Experimental WebKit Features**

- Re-put On **Blank anchor target implies...** activation button.
- Re-put On **Fetch API Request KeepAlive ...** activation button.
- Re-put On **Quirk to prevent delayed initial pain...** activation button.
- Re-put On **Intersection Observer...** activation button.
- Re-put On **Media Capabilities Extensions** activation button.
- Re-put On **Pointer Events** activation button.
- Re-put On **Swap Processes on Cross-Site...** activation button.
- Re-put On **Synthetic Editing Commands** activation button.
- Re-put On **Block top-level redirects by third...** activation button.
- Re-put On the **Visual Viewport API** activation button.
- Re-put On **WebRTC H264 Simulcast** activation button.
- Re-put On **WebRTC mDNS ICE Candidates** activation button.
- Re-put On **WebRTC Unified Plan** activation button.
- Re-put On the **WebRTC VP8** activation button.
- Re-put On **Disable Web SQL** activation button.

GUIDE EIGHT

How You Can Fully Use Camera and Photo Apps on Your iPhone Professionally

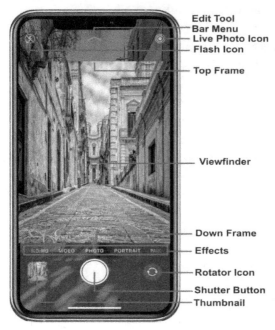

Camera app could be used to locate and get all your recent snapped photos through Thumbnail and take pictures of every image around you. The Camera app contains features that will enable you to take a live picture and modified compressed Panorama images. All the captured photographs are automatically saved in Photo Library.

In the Camera interface, you will see options that can be used to take different pictures and what you can do to add more lovely effect to the pictures.

iPhone Camera is an advanced camera that could be used to snap flowering plants, animals, human and nonliving things at the back and front of your iPhone by tapping on the Camera rotating icon which "I called Camera Rotator" that can change the back facing Camera to front-facing Camera to take Selfie.

The different modes in your Camera are including Video, Time-Lapse, Slo-Mo, Pano (Panorama), Portrait, and Photo Mode.

When your iPhone iOS 13 is upgraded to iOS 13.2 and above you will see a more beneficial feature like Deep Fusion.

To add more lovely effects to your picture, you can use Filter, Night Mode, Live Photo, and Burst.

What You Can See On the Camera Screen

1. Flash Icon: It is at the top left angle of the screen.
2. Night Mode Icon: It is located by the immediate side of the Flash.
3. Live Photo Icon: It is located at the top right angle of the screen.
4. Edit Toolbar Menu Icon: It is located at the top center of the screen.
5. View Frame: It is located at the center of the screen where the image will appear.
6. Zoom Range: It is at the base of the View Frame to adjust the size of your image.
7. Camera Modes in Row: It is at the top of the Shutter frame.
8. Thumbnail: It is at the left bottom of the screen to show a newly snapped image.
9. Shutter Button: It is at the bottom center of the screen to snap image(s).
10. Camera Rotator Icon: It is at the bottom right of the screen.

There various ways you can access Camera on your iPhone.

Lock-Screen

➢ Slide your iPhone screen from the right side to the left at the Lock-screen.
➢ Hit on the **Camera icon** at the bottom right of the iPhone screen.

Homescreen

> Hit on the **Camera Icon**
> Position the Camera to pace the image at the center of the View Screen.
> Hit on the **Shutter** or Up or Down Volume Button on the left side of your iPhone.

For You To Secure Your Photograph

Homescreen: Hit on **Setting Icon**

Settings: Select **Camera**

Camera: Select **Preserve Settings**

Preserve Settings: Put On the **Live Photo, Camera Mode,** and **Creative Control** Activators.

How Your iPhone Camera Could Be Used to Scan Quick Response (QR) Code

You can effectively use your iPhone Camera to scan the information on Quick Response (QR) Code by initially going to the Setting to activate the scanning feature activator.

This will allow you to go to a website without you typing the *web address* on your iPhone browser **web tab** of Safari.

How to Activate the Camera QR Code Scanner

Homescreen: Hit on the **Settings** icon.

Settings: Select **Camera**

Camera

> Hit on the **Scan QR Code** activation switch to activate it.

  . The switch will change from white to green.
> Swipe Up to go back to Homescreen.

136

How you can use the Camera App to Scan the QR Code on your iPhone

Lock Screen or Homescreen or Control Center: Hit on the **Camera icon**

Camera

> ➢ Ensure that you are using the Rear (Back) Camera. If not, hit on Camera turning icon (rotator) [icon] at the bottom right of the screen to turn the camera view to the rear Camera.
> ➢ Position your camera to focus on the Quick Response Code.
> ➢ A notification will show up on your screen for you to open the **Website** link (e.g. Open "amazon.com" in Safari).

Notification

WEBSITE QR CODE
Open "amazon.com" in Safari

> ➢ Hit on the notification to open the website link with the **Quick Response**.

How You Can Make Clear & Quality Pictures in a Dark Environment

To prevent night defect on your photograph you have to make use of **Flash and Night Mode** Features to completely remove shadow or reflection of darkness on your picture outcome.

Look at the top left side of the Camera interface you will see Flash and Night mode of the screen; hit on the Flash to see select "ON" and also hit on Night Mode to change to yellow (ACTIVE appearance).

When you re-touch the Flash and Night Mode they will be UNACTIVE that is, they will stop working.

Night Mode: Your iPhone will automatically show Night Mode to control the light around the image when the surrounding is dark.

Photo Taking

You can take photos in a portrait by positioning your iPhone in the normal vertical position ▮ or landscape ▬ by making the iPhone to be positioned in a horizontal position (i.e. move the iPhone long side in 45° to ground level).

Homescreen: Hit on **Camera Icon**

Camera

- ➤ Hit on **PHOTO**
- ➤ Position the Camera either in Portrait or in Landscape.
- ➤ Let the image be at the center of Camera View.
- ➤ Hit the **Shutter** or click any of the Volume buttons at the side of your iPhone.
- ➤ You will see the photo in the **Thumbnail** below.
- ➤ Hit on the **Thumbnail** to review the Photo.
- ➤ You may also go to the Photo app to select your snapped picture.
- ➤ **To Delete:** Hit on Photo App and hit on all the pictures you want to delete and hit on **Waste Bin** at the bottom right of the screen.

Portrait Photo

It is an amazing invention of Photo modification the can make your Photo come out in various professional light to enhance the quality of the image.

The loaded lights are Natural, Studio, Contour, Stage, Stage Light Mono, and High-Key Light Mono respectively.

- ➤ Look at the lower base of the View Frame scroll from either left to right or right to left to hit on **PORTRAIT.**
- ➤ Once you position your iPhone in Portrait the various light will show above the lower region of the View frame in arc direction.
- ➤ Hit the ball one by one to see its light effect on the image. Scroll toward the left to see the rest of the light.
- ➤ Let your image be either automatic focus (rectangular) at the center of the Viewfinder or hit any location on the screen to make your focus point.
- ➤ Hit on Shutter to snap the image. You can also do the same for yourself.

Pano Mode (Panorama)

Homescreen: Hit on **Camera Icon**

Camera Interface

- ➤ Look at the lower base of the View Frame scroll from either left to right or right to left to hit on **Pano.**
- ➤ First, let the Camera capture the left end of the image.
- ➤ View it in the rectangle Image View
- ➤ Hit on Shutter to start capture
- ➤ Slowly move your hand straight from the left edge side of the Image to the right edge side of the image. Use the Arrow on a straight line to guide your straight movement.
- ➤ Hit on the same Shutter to stop the shot.
- ➤ The Image will be spherically wide in size and look beautiful.
- ➤ You can also use it to make Selfies in the same method.

Live Photo

Homescreen: Hit on **Camera Icon**

- ➤ Look at the lower base of the View Frame scroll from either left to right or right to left to select **Photo**

➢ Hit on the **Live** icon at the top right side of the Camera interface, the icon will change to yellow and you will see LIVE at the top center of the page.

➢ Let the Camera capture image correctly within a rectangle that is automatically showing at the center of the view fame.

➢ Hit on Shutter to take a shot of the image.

➢ The Image will be saved in the Photo library as Live Photo.

Zoom Capture

The Zoom sizes are shown at the lower base of the View Frame. If the image you want to capture is very small in the **Camera View** you can hit on either time 1 or times 2 to enlarge the image on your screen.

Finger Method

You can place your thumb and a finger on the screen and move them away from each other to enlarge the image or pitching the screen to reduce the image. When you move the two fingers together it will reduce the image size.

Add Effect on a Saved Photo in the Library

➢ Camera Interface: Look at the bottom left of the Camera you will see a small rectangle show image, it is called **Thumbnail**.

➢ It the **Thumbnail** to view the recent image on the screen. Swipe from right to left to see more pictures you have shot before.

➢ Stop at the image you want to edit.

➢ Look at the top center you will see a menu minimized arrowhead which is called **Edit Menu** ⌃.

- ➢ Hit on the **Menu Toolbar** for a dropdown of different Edit options will appear.
- ➢ Select **Filter** and you will see the chosen image appear in different thumbnails with different color effects on each image replicate.
- ➢ Select the one like.
- ➢ Hit on **Done** to save the selected image.

Add Effect on the Captured Image

- ➢ Camera Interface: Look at the top center you will see a menu minimized arrowhead ⬡ which is called **Edit Menu.**
- ➢ Hit on the **Menu Toolbar** for a dropdown of different Edit options will appear.
- ➢ Select **Filter** and you will see different thumbnails with different color attractions. ⬤
- ➢ Scroll from right to left and select any of the thumbnails with lovely color influence. The color will transform the image and the environment look.
- ➢ Hit on Shutter to take your shot.
- ➢ The newly captured image will be seen in the bottom left **Thumbnail**.

Use Burst Shot for Multiple Photo Shots at a Goal

It will enable you to take a continuous photo shot that you can later select the nice pictures among the total shots.

- ➢ Camera Interface: Let your iPhone Camera be positioned at the image.
- ➢ Use your finger to move the **Shutter** to the left without you lifting your finger till you complete all the number of **Burst Shots** you wanted to take at a time.
- ➢ The Camera will continually snap the image.
- ➢ Remove your finger from the Shutter, for it to return to the center and stop the continuous shots.

Video Recording

The Video mode is similar to Slo-Mo processes. The output of the Video will be accurate with the original movement without any delay.

To have the best of the Normal Video and Slo-Mo Video production on your iPhone with the highest quality resolution you have to initially do the following regulation in the Settings before you start the recording.

Homescreen: Hit on **Settings Icon**

Settings: Select **Camera**

Camera: Hit on **Record SLO-MO**

> **Record SLO-MO:** Select **1080p HD** at **240fps** (frame per second), return to **Camera** settings by hitting on **Back Icon** at the top left of the screen

Camera: Hit on **Record Video**

> **Record Video**

> ➢ Select **4k at 60fps.**
> ➢ Hit on **Back Icon** to return to **Camera** settings.

Camera: Hit on **Format**

> **Format:** Hit on **High Efficiency**

➢ Return to the **Homescreen.**

Homescreen: Hit on **Camera App Icon**

Camera Interface

➢ Select **Video** from the Camera Modes below the View margin.
➢ Hit on the Red Recording Button to **Start** the recording.
➢ Hit on the button again to Stop the **Video Recording.**

142

Slo-Mo (Slow Motion)

You can apply motion with a timer to beautify modeling, sports activities, production stages, advertisement, growth... and many others.

Camera Interface: Below the View-frame scroll the Camera mode and hit on **Slo-Mo**.

➢ Position your iPhone either in Portrait or Landscape the best way you want it.
➢ Hit on the Red Recording Button at the bottom center to start your either **Selfie Slo-Mo** or Scene/Event/Action taking place at the front of your Camera.
➢ Hit on the Red Recording Button again to Stop the **Slo-Mo Recording.**
➢ **To Play Your Recorded Slo-Mo:** Go to Homescreen and hit on **Photo App.**
➢ Hit on the **Slo-Mo** and it will play. You can share with your friends in iMessage, Social Media by tapping **Share Icon** at the bottom of the screen.

How You Can Use Professional Camera App To Boost Your Photograph Quality

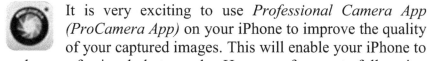 It is very exciting to use *Professional Camera App (ProCamera App)* on your iPhone to improve the quality of your captured images. This will enable your iPhone to produce professional photographs. However, for you to fully enjoy the benefits of the ProCamera App then you will need to know how to control the Picture's Manual Shutter Speed, ISO, Exposure... and many others, for you to get an amazing outstanding picture(s)

To start with, you have to download an additional Camera App called **ProCamera** that will enable you to have access to a menu that contains many editing tools you could use to improve the general quality of the Photo.

When you launch the ProCamera App, it will show the normal Camera App look with advanced feature of exposure control under Viewfinder for you to regulate the picture exposure to be brighter or darker when you place your finger on the **Zero (O)** Calibrated Pointer and slide the control pointer toward the right to increase the exposure brightness or toward the left to increase the exposure darkness.

How to Access Professional Menu

After you have downloaded ProCamera on your iPhone.

Homescreen: Hit on ProCamera App.

On the Camera Interface: Look at the bottom left of the screen to hit on the **Menu icon.** ☰

The hidden menu will display all the available advanced effect tools for you to use.

Hit on any of the icons on the menu. It will show the icon and its features on the Camera screen.

The Menu contains:

1. Rapid Fire

2. F/E (Focus Point and Exposure) Locked

144

3. Grids ⊞

4. Tiltmeter ⊕

5. ISO & Shutter Ⓜ

6. White Balance 🆆🅱

7. Histogram

8. Aspect Ratio

9. JPEG Format

10. Anti-Shake

11. Self Timer

12. Standard

13. Settings ◉

1. **Rapid Fire:** The feature of Rapid Fire is the same as the feature of the Burst method of taking many pictures within a very short time by pressing and hold the Shutter.

ProCamera Menu

➢ Hit on the Menu icon
➢ Hit on the **Rapid Fire** icon
➢ Go down to the bottom right of the menu to tap on the Menu icon. This will hide all the menu effect tools.
➢ Position your Camera to the Image you want to snap, press, and hold the Shutter to snap the number of shots you want.

2. **Focus Point and Exposure (E/F) Lock:** This feature is used to lock the focus point and exposure level you preferred for the picture.

- ➤ Position your Camera to the image you want to snap.
- ➤ Hit the surface of the Viewfinder for both Focus Point and Exposure Shapes to appear on the screen.
- ➤ On the Viewfinder, you will see focus points in a square shape and exposure in a circular shape. With the use of your finger move the square shape to the area that should be sharp on the viewfinder, and move the circle to the area where the exposure is needed to be corrected.
- ➤ Use the control below to regulate the exposure and the focus as you move your finger on the controlling panel.
- ➤ Hit on the Menu icon at the bottom right of the screen to display the editing tools.
- ➤ Select F/E Lock icon
- ➤ Hit on Menu icon at the bottom right to hide the effect tools.
- ➤ Now you can move your Camera anywhere and how to capture different shots without any irregularity.
- ➤ As soon as you have finished taking Photos go to the menu and hit on the **F/E Lock** icon to disable it. The **F/E Lock** icon will appear white when it is disabled but lemon green when it is enabled (active).

Hint: If you move your Camera before you select **F/E Lock** from the Menu the focus and exposure setting will change.

3. **Grids:** The advanced grids are more compact than the grids in the ordinary Camera App. It can be used to centralize a very small image that could not be done with the other grids on the Camera app.

- ➤ Hit on the Menu icon at the bottom right
- ➤ Select **Grids** icon
- ➤ Hit on the Menu icon
- ➤ Use the squares on the viewfinder to set your image.
- ➤ Hit on Shutter to take the Picture.

➤ You can go back to Menu to disable the active Grids icon.

4. **Tiltmeter:** This will enable you to balance the Camera of your iPhone. The cross icon shows if the image is correctly positioned.

ProCamera Menu

➤ Hit on the Menu icon at the bottom right
➤ Select **Tiltmeter** icon
➤ Hit on the Menu icon
➤ Use the Tiltmeter (Big Cross) on the viewfinder to be in line with the small cross and when it is correctly registered on each other the Tiltmeter will turn to **Green**.
➤ Hit on Shutter to take the Picture.
➤ You can go back to Menu to disable the active Tiltmeter icon.

5. **ISO & Shutter**: This is also called **Manual Mode** that regulates the speed of Shutter and could be used to control exposure as it is used in Digital Single-Len Reflex Camera.
The faster the Shutter the more the advantage of producing a clearer picture with low light.
The higher the number of ISO the more light-sensitive your iPhone Camera.

ProCamera Menu

➤ Hit on the **Menu icon** at the bottom right
➤ Select **ISO & Shutter** icon
➤ Hit on the Menu icon
➤ At the top of the Viewfinder, you will see Shutter Speed reading rate **1/3xxx s** and **ISO 4x.** Tap on 1/3xxx
➤ Use the Shutter Speed to control the speed time.

To Control ISO

> ➢ Hit on the **ISO 4x** (e.g ISO 48) at the top right of the Viewfinder.
> ➢ Drag the **ISO Sensitivity Regulator** below the Viewfinder toward the right to increase your iPhone Camera light sensitivity.

6. **White Balance:** The Picture colors on your Camera are controlled by color temperature which is known as additional Blue that is representing Cooler and additional Yellow which is representing Warmer. If you add more of yellow color to your picture that means it is having additional warming temperature while the increase of Blue color on your picture is reducing the temperature of your picture and the temperature is reading in **Kelvin (K)**

ProCamera Menu

> ➢ Hit on the **Menu** icon at the bottom right
> ➢ Select the **White Balance** icon
> ➢ Hit on the Menu icon
> ➢ At the bottom of the Viewfinder hit on **AWB** the reading scale will show.
> ➢ The cooling (Blue) temperature is increasing when you move the Color Temperature Slider toward the left while Warming (Yellow) temperature is increasing when you move the slider toward the right.

Hint: As you are adding blue the temperature reading value will be reducing and as you are adding yellow to the picture the temperature reading value will be increasing.

7. **Histogram**: This is a picture graph that explains the equal exposure level of darkness or brightness pixels on a Picture. It shows if a

picture is having high or excessive brightness (i.e. overexposure) or darkness (i.e. underexposure).

ProCamera Menu

- ➢ Hit on the **Menu** icon at the bottom right
- ➢ Select **Histogram** icon
- ➢ Hit on the Menu icon

Hint: The right peak side of the picture exposure graph is representing the maximum brightness pixels in the picture.

The middle area of the picture color graph is showing a minimal level of brightness.

The left peak side of the picture exposure graph is representing the optimal level of darkness.

When you either reduce or add exposure to your picture through the use of Exposure Compensation, It will quickly arrange the histogram to show the effects of the picture color pixels.

For You to Remove the Histograph

- ➢ Hit on the **Menu** icon at the bottom right
- ➢ Hit on the **Histogram** icon to deactivate it. It will change from lemon green to white.
- ➢ Hit on the Menu icon to minimize the editing tools.

8. **Anti-Shake:** As the name implies, it prevents the image capture from going through an unconscious and uncontrollable shaking defect when the light is low or poor. It ensures clear and sharp capture of images in a poor light environment.

Anti-Shake will automatically switch on itself as soon as the Camera discovered the surrounding light is bad for a good picture. When you launch the **ProCamera App** and go to Menu, you will

149

see the Anti-Shake feature has been automatically switched On to ensure quality Photo.

9. Aspect Ratio: This is an interesting ProCamera feature that helps all individuals to print out their photos according to the size of their desirable Photo's Frame.

The ratio measures the breadth and height of the Photo you are about to take. By default, you will see 3:2 on your Camera when you have activated the Aspect Ratio option on the menu.

This option is telling you that the size of the Photo breadth will be 3 while the height will be 2.

Practically, if you want to choose a frame, you will need to understand how to work out the Aspect Ratio first.

Ratio 3:2 means, the breadth is taking the size of 3 out of 5 (3/5 or three-fifth) and the height is taking the size of 2 out of 5 (2/5 or two-fifth)

If you are having the size of the frame, you must calculate the ratio between the breath and the height of the frame.

For instance, 4 inches by 6 inches Frame size

In this contest, a small number (4) comes before the bigger number (6). Any of the sides could be considered breadth or height since the difference between them is ratio 3:2.

How can you know that?

Continue dividing both figures with a common number that could go in them until you are unable to divide them again a common number.

Between 4 and 6 the common number for both is 2

Divide both by 2 = 4/2 = 2; and 6/2 = 3

150

Now you can conclude that the frame is ratio 2:3 is the same with ratio 3:2.

Let's try another frame size 16 inches by 24 inches (16" x 24")

What are the common numbers (also called a common factor) in both?

Start from the smallest number: 2,4, & 8

Those three numbers could completely divide both sides to last the last number that could not allow any division again.

To safe time, let's use 8

If you divide both numbers by 8 you will get = 16/8 =2; and 24/8 = 3

The fame 16" x 24" is in Aspect Ratio 2:3.

Therefore, the frame could work perfectly for any picture you have taken with an Aspect Ratio 3:2

Now, you can try to find out the ratio of these frame sizes.

1. 8" x 12"
2. 32" x 48" and
3. 64" x 96"

I wish you good luck.

ProCamera Menu

You can change the Aspect Ratio from default ratio 3:2 to another commonly available of your own choice by tapping on the **Aspect Ratio** icon in the ProCamera Menu.

Every each time you tap the Aspect Ratio it will change to another option of the ratio which includes:

1. 1:1
2. 3:1 Panorama Size.
3. 4:3

4. 5:4
5. 16:9
6. Golden Mean

10. File Format: This will help you to compress your pictures to use very small storage space on your iPhone & iCloud when the pictures are saved in JPG/JPEG format.

Ordinarily, your Camera always saves your Photographs in JPEG format to make them compatible and very useful in all devices.

Although, JPEG pictures are compressed photos, meanwhile, in the process of compressing and saving the pictures in JPEG format they partially lose some degree of light which affects the overall quality. However, they are still pretty good to use.

But, with the use of the **ProCamera App** on your iPhone you can effectively use other options of saving your pictures. The other options are TIFF, RAW, and RAW+JPEG.

These options will not compress your Photos as a result, they will be very heavy and take too much of storage space on your iPhone and iCloud.

The advantage is that any picture you save with either TIFF or RAW will 100% protect the degree of the light, total exposure, and come out excellently.

How to select the File Format of Your Choice

You may want to save a particular picture in a different file format based on a special request. Take the steps below:

ProCamera Menu

> Hit on the **Menu** icon at the bottom right

➤ Hit on **File Format**, you will first see JPEF; re-tap the icon you will see TIFF and continue tapping it till you see your preferred option.
➤ Hit on the Menu icon
➤ When you are through, go back to the menu to reset it to the JPEG file.

GUIDE NINE

How You Can Protect You iPhone 11 with Strong IDs' Security

How You Can Create a Protective Apple ID Successfully

Apple ID will protect your vital documents, Apple Pay Credit Card; it will enable you to buy more applications on your iPhone, create more lively activities, activation, or settings of different apps… and many others.

You need to have one iPhone ID to link all your Apple devices like Apple iPhones, iPads, Macbook, iMac, Mac, and Watch together. That is if you are privileged to have more than one same or different types of Apple's devices.

How To Create Your Apple ID Process

1. Homescreen Approach the Settings Icon by hitting on it.
2. Settings: Look at the side of Profile Picture at the top and hit on **Sign In to Your iPhone.**
3. Apple ID
   ➢ In the Email text field, type your active **Email Address**.
   ➢ Look at the top right angle of the screen to tap on **Next.**
   ➢ Hit on an option of Don't Have An Apple ID
   ➢ You will see an informative box with **Create Apple ID.** Tap on the option.
4. Date of Birth
   ➢ Type in your **Date of Birth** in the provided text field.
   ➢ At the top angle of the screen hit on **Next.**
5. Name: Provide your **Name and Last Name** into the text field and hit on **Next.**
6. Email

- ➤ Make sure you enter the initial **Email** without typographical mistake or choose to **Get Free iCloud Email Address** and hit on the **Next** option.
- ➤ If you choose **Free iCloud Email** tap on **Next** and **Continue.**

Password

- ➤ You will be allowed two times to type your **Password.** Type the same password in the first password text field into the second verify password text field. If incorrect it won't continue.
- ➤ Make eight and above digits of a password that can comprise of a number, uppercase, and lowercase alphabetical letters.
- ➤ Hit **Next** at the top to continue.

7. Phone Number
- ➤ Carefully choose your Country
- ➤ Type your **Phone Number** for your identity verification.

8. Verification Method: Select any of the below options:
- ➤ **Text Message**
- ➤ **Phone Call**
- ➤ Confirm your option with **Checkmark** and hit on **Next**

9. Security Questions
- ➤ Give an unforgettable answer to the security question you will be asked. You can write the question and the answer into your confidential

155

organizer/planner to subsequently guide you in giving the exact answer whenever you are asked the same question during an essential activity on your iPhone.

10.

11. Verification Code

➢ Type the **Text 6-Digits Code** sent to you through your iPhone Message into the **Verification designated space** for the **Code.**

12. Terms and Conditions

➢ Read through the terms and conditions, digest, and get used to them or familiarize yourself with them because it is very important and hit on **Agree.** If you **Disagree,** that implies that you are not in support of Apple's Terms and Conditions guiding the Apple ID ownership as a result the Apple ID process will be discontinued /terminated.

13. Enter iPhone Passcode: Type your iPhone **Passcode** (4 or 6 digits). If you do not have a passcode, go to the **Add Passcode** page on the section to learn how to create your iPhone Passcode.

14. iCloud

➢ There will be a need for iCloud to get documents from Contact, Reminder, Notes, Calendar, and Safari on your iPhone.

156

Therefore, hit on the **Merge** option.

➢ You may consider the other option of **Don't Merge** if you are having any otherwise opinion on their synchronization.

15. Find My iPhone Box

➢ On the box accept by tapping on **OK.**

Hint: You will see your Full Name appear where you saw Sign in to Your iPhone. Anytime you want to sign in to your iPhone hit on your Name and continue.

Now, you have created an Apple ID for yourself. Please you need to keep email & password details carefully to prevent false operators or fraudsters using your iPhone for illegal activities.

How To Change Your Apple ID Process

Homescreen: Approach the Settings Icon by hitting on it.

Settings: Look at the Profile Name beside Profile Picture at the top hit on **Name.**

Password & Security

➢ Hit on **Change Password**
➢ Type in your valid **Password.**
➢ Type in your **New Password**
➢ Type in your **New Password** again for confirmation
➢ Hit on **Change Password**

How To Sign In Apple ID On Your iPhone Process

Homescreen: Approach the Settings Icon by hitting on it.

Settings: Look at the Profile Name beside Profile Picture at the top hit on **Sign In to Your iPhone.**

Apple ID

> In the Email text field, type your active **Email Address**.
> Look at the top right angle of the screen to hit on **Next.**
> In the Password text field type in complex and easy to remember **Password.** Better still write it into your confidential organizer.
> Look at the top right angle of the screen to tap on **Next.**
> In the last part of the page, you will see Sign Out and hit on it to leave the page.

Now, you have added your Apple ID on your iPhone.

How To Recover Your Forgot Apple ID Process

Homescreen: Approach the **Settings Icon** by hitting on it.

Settings: Look at the Profile Name beside Profile Picture at the top hit on **Sign In to Your iPhone.**

Apple ID:

> First and foremost, type your correct Email add into the email text field.
> Look below you will see a 2-in-1 question state thus, Don't have an Apple ID or Forgot it?
> Hit on **Forgot it.**
> **On Informative Box** hit on **Forgot Apple ID.**
> Firstly, you will type in a new

Password and secondly type the same password for the system to verify the correctness.

➢ Go to the top right angle of the screen to tap on **Next.**

You can verify it by tapping on Sign In, Type your submitted email, tap next, type your new approved Password, and tap next.

How to Make Your Face ID Successfully on Your iPhone 11

Face ID is another defensive mechanism/tool you can use to prevent fake users from using your iPhone. The use of Face ID on your iPhone will strongly enhance your iPhone security. It can be used to Unlock your iPhone.

You can use Face ID to buy things from iTunes Store, Apple Store, Apple Book with the use of your Apple pay.

Face ID in these modern developed iPhones X has replaced Touch ID in the lower iPhones, as a result, you will see Face ID & Passcode together under Settings on your new iPhone not Touch ID & Passcode.

But, it is less effective among the identical twins that are physically looking alike. It will be difficult for your iPhone Face ID infrared sensor to identify or differentiate the facially identical people.

How You Can Create Face ID via Settings Process

Homescreen: Approach the **Settings Icon** by hitting on it.

Settings: Search down to hit on **Set Up Face ID.**

Camera

➢ The Camera should be positioned in a portrait to capture your face. Don't allow any other person to stay behind you when you are taking your face.
➢ Hit on the "**Get Started**" bar.
➢ Let your face be boldly covered in the Camera view center.

159

➤ Focus your eyes on the Front-Facing Camera Sensor and let your head be in the middle of the round frame on the screen.

➤ As you are turning your head gradually the surrounding lines of the round frame will be changing to green, keep turning your head and let every side of your head be captured by the Camera sensor till the surrounding lines are completely changed to green.

➤ If the first Face ID scanner is successful, hit on the **Continue** bar and turn your head in either the same or opposite way again, once the second Face ID scanner is complete, hit on **Done** bar.

Hint: If you are unable to turn your head or stiff neck, hit on **Accessibility.**

How You Can Make A Protective Passcode on Your iPhone 11

Most of the time your iPhone will always ask you to create a personal Passcode to alternate Face ID to unlock your iPhone. In a situation that you are having an identical twin-face that the Face ID may compromise, you should have a Passcode that is only known to you, then you can use the Passcode to prevent your twin from accessing your iPhone without your consent.

In a situation whereby the Face ID failed to identify your face because of the face transformation you applied (i.e. face mask, excessive face makeup, etc.) then automatically your iPhone will request for your iPhone instead.

Surely, your iPhone will ask for Passcode anytime you perform the below tasks on your iPhone:

➤ For Installation of iOS
➤ Restarting or Switching On of Your iPhone.
➤ To Remove/Delete All The Data on Your iPhone.
➤ To Change or Access Passcode Settings on Your iPhone.

➢ To Perform Software Update.

How You Can Create Passcode via Settings Process

Homescreen: Approach the **Settings Icon** by hitting on it.

Settings: Search down the page and select the **Face ID & Passcode** option.

Face ID & Passcode

➢ Search down the page hit on **Turn Passcode On** option.
➢ By default, you will see 6 digits passcode which you can change to a 4-digits passcode.
➢ But, if you are comfortable with the 6-digits type, then input complex **Passcode** that will have the mixture of Number, Small Case, and Capital Case of Alphabets.
➢ For 4-digits Passcode, hit on **Passcode Options** above the Keyboard and tap on the third option.
  ✓ A Custom Alphanumeric Code
  ✓ A Custom Numeric Code
  ✓ **4-Digit Numeric Code**
➢ Re-type the complex Passcode for confirmation

Hint: You have to make your Passcode to be complex to prevent passcode hackers or guessers from predicting your passcode. Therefore, mix the passcode digits by selecting **Alphanumeric Code** and write it on your planner for record purposes.

Have you suspected that your present Passcode has been exposed to the wrong person?

Are you noticing suspicious operations on your iPhone?

Then, take a protective wise approach by changing the present passcode to a new Passcode.

How You Can Change Insecure Passcode

Homescreen: Hit on **Settings Icon**.

Settings: Search down the page and select the **Face ID & Passcode** option.

Face ID & Passcode: Search down the page and hit on **Change Passcode** option.

Change Passcode:

> ➢ If you are using 6 or 4-Digits Password, type the insecure Password.
> ➢ The New Passcode will be requested to be re-typed twice.

Once you type the last digit, it will automatically approve and move to the previous page.

How You Can Activation of Apps in iCloud Account

The activation of apps in the iCloud account will determine the number of apps data that will be automatically uploaded and stored in iCloud storage for you to access them from all your devices. There are lots of suggested apps on your iPhone you can backup and store in the iCloud storage.

This can only be done if you switch on those apps on the iCloud page. Follow the below steps to select the appropriate apps that you want to back up with iCloud.

Therefore, you have to make more storage space available on your iPhone.

The example of the Apps is *Photo, Mail, Contacts, Calendars, Reminders, Notes, Messages, Safari, News, Stocks, Home, Health, Wallet, Game Center, and Siri.*

Homescreen: Approach the **Settings Icon** by hitting on it.

Settings: Look at the Profile Name beside Profile Picture at the top hit on **Sign In to Your iPhone.**

Apple ID: Look at the middle of the page and hit on the **iCloud** option.

iCloud: Hit the apps activation switch to change the switch look to green appearance.

Keychain:

> ➢ Hit on **Keychain** to turn "On" the **iCloud Keychain** switch.
> ➢ Return to the iCloud page by tapping on the **Back Arrow of iCloud** at the top left angle of the screen.

Hint: In all the devices you are using, it will constantly retain the credit card details and password you have accepted.

Find My iPhone

> ➢ Select **Find My iPhone** below the Keychain option under iCloud.
> ➢ Hit on **Find My iPhone** switch to activate it.
> ➢ Return to the iCloud page by tapping on the **Back Arrow of iCloud** at the top left angle of the screen.

Hint: This will enable you to locate, lock, activate, or erase your iPhone and other approved equipment if you produce your **Password**.

iCloud Backup

> ➢ Select **iCloud Backup** option
> ➢ Hit on **iCloud Backup** to activate the backup.
> ➢ Return to the iCloud page by tapping on the **Back Arrow of iCloud** at the top left angle of the screen.

iCloud Drive: It will accept all apps to store data and documents in iCloud.

> ➢ Hit on **iCloud Drive** to activate it.

➢ Move to the top left of the page to tap on the **Back icon** of Apple ID.

Hit on the **Back icon** at the top of Settings and swipe up from the center bottom of the iPhone to go back to the Homescreen.

GUIDE TEN

How You Can Find Your Lost iPhone 11

There are some important steps of settings that you have to do on your iPhone which will make the feature of **Find My** active on your iPhone 11.

1. Find Friends and Family Members or
2. Share your location with others
3. Set up **Find My.**

How You Can Activate **Find My** on Your iPhone

Hint: **"Find My"** is automatically turned on when you Sign In your new iPhone with your Apple ID, but, there is a need for you to find out if **Find My iPhone, Enable Offline Finding** and **Send Last Location** are activated.

Homescreen: Hit on **Settings**

Settings: Hit on your **Name/Sign In To Your iPhone** beside the profile picture.

Apple ID: Hit on **Find My**

Find My

➢ Hit on **Find My iPhone** to select **"On"** if the activation

165

feature is **Off.**

Find My iPhone: Turn On the activators of the following if they are Off:

- ✓ **Find My iPhone:** It will always request your Password to locate, erase, or lock your iPhone.
- ✓ **Enable Offline Finding:** Your iPhone will be located even when it is not connected to a Cellular or Wi-Fi network.
- ✓ **Send Last Location:** iCloud will automatically send the location of your iPhone to Apple when the battery is drastically low.
- ➢ Hit on **My Location** to select **This Device.**
- ➢ Hit on **Share My Location's** Activator to put On the switch.

What To Do After You Have Lost Your iPhone

There is a possibility of misplacing your iPhone 11 in a location that you could not recollect because you had visited more than three places before you could remember that your iPhone is missing or it was stolen by a thief.

Also, you might have kept the iPhone in a compartment that is best known to you only but after a while, you could not remember specifically where exactly you had hidden the iPhone.

However, Apple has made a reliable way of locating your iPhone 11 with the use of Find My iPhone and iCloud Map Detection or Google Map to specifically describe and identify the location of your iPhone 11 wherever it had been kept.

First Finding Solution

On Mac or PC

- ➢ Use any of the available browsers such as Chrome, Mozilla Firefox, Internet Explorer, Safari, Opera, Lynx, or Konqueror.
- ➢ In the Web Add text field type **icloud.com.**

iCloud Homepage:

➤ Sign In with your Apple ID which includes your **Email** and **Password**.

➤ Click on **Find iPhone Icon**  among the icons on the screen.

iCloud Find My iPhone: Location Map will display on the screen.

➤ At the top **bar** center of the screen click on All Devices.

➤ On the **drop-down & select your iPhone**. (If you are using more than one Apple device that is using the same Apple ID. You will see all the Apple devices on the drop-down).

➤ The Map will zoom out to indicate the iPhone location with a black circle and your iPhone' Name label

➤ At the right corner, you will see 3 options you can use to help your findings

✓ Play Sound
✓ Lost Mode
✓ Erase iPhone

Play Sound: If you pretty sure that the iPhone is around (home, workshop, or office) then you can click **Play Sound** immediately you will start hearing vibration with sound. The sound will continue until you hit on **Find My iPhone Alert OK**.

Lost Mode: This option perfect when you discovered that you can no longer recover/find your iPhone again then you can click on **Lost Mode.**

✓ **Phone Number Dialog Box:** Type your **Phone Number** (that can be called by the finder) and click on **Next** at the top right corner of the dialog box.

✓ Click on the Text box, type the message that will be shown on your iPhone 11 screen. e.g. **"Please I have lost this iPhone. Kindly Call Me. Thank you"** and click on **Done** at the top right angle of the dialog box.

Automatically the iPhone will be locked. It will only be unlocked if you enter your passcode or through your Face ID.

Erase iPhone: This option is accurate when you realized that the iPhone could not be located, then, click **Erase iPhone** to completely remove all your vital and confidential **data, applications (apps) & documents** from the iPhone quickly.

Second Finding Solution:

This is can be used when you are having Google Map App on your iPhone but if do not have the app you can use the iCloud method above.

On Mac or PC

➢ Use any of the available browsers such as Chrome, Mozilla Firefox, Internet Explorer, Safari, Opera, Lynx, or Konqueror.

➢ In the Web Add text field type **www.google.com/maps**

Google Maps:

➢ Click on **Menu Icon** at the top left side of the **Search Google Maps Text Field**.

➢ **Menu:** Select **Your Timeline** (Timeline will show various locations you have been with your iPhone on Google maps with an indication of red color).

➢ At the to left side of the screen click on **Today** at the front of the **Timeline**.

Immediately a line will displace your different movement today on the Google maps to know where your iPhone could be found.

➢ You can zoom in the map to make the location to be closer and clearer for you to see the location very well.

➢ You can increase the displacement line (appear in blue) at the left side of the screen to see more of different places with their specific time in hours, minutes, and seconds that you moved from a particular place to another place till the final place where the iPhone could be found.

Note: You won't see the exact spot where the iPhone could be found on the Google map but you could only know the environment where you can see the iPhone.

google.com/maps
On Your Computer
Step 1

Step 2

Menu
Top Left of the Page
Step 3

Google Maps

~Your Timeline

Step 4

TODAY

Step 5

169

How You Can Use Another iPhone to Track

Your Lost iPhone

The method of tracking your lost iPhone on the computer is virtually the same with the method and processes of locating your lost iPhone on another iPhone.

If you are having two iPhones in your family or your friend is have one, you can easily use the available iPhone to quickly discover where your iPhone is kept or the location at which it could be found with either hope of recovery or not.

Homescreen: Hit on **Find My** App Icon

Find My: Hit on **Devices** icon at the bottom center of your iPhone.

Devices: Hit on your lost **iPhone 11's Name** (e.g. Ephong's iPhone) that is your first name will be used to qualified the lost iPhone.

iPhone 11's Name: Swipe up from the top edge center of the page to select one of the available options below:

1. **Play Sound**: Having 100% assurance of finding it.
2. **Directions**: If it is discovered on the map and you want it to be tracked down,
3. **Notifications:** You will be

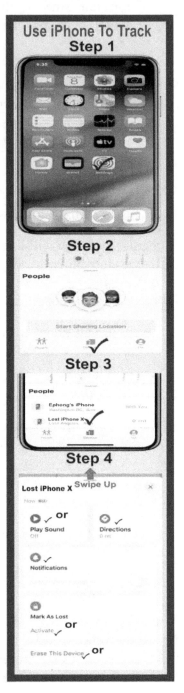

notified when the iPhone is found.

4. **Mark As Lost**: If the recovery chances of your iPhone is 70 – 80% but the location on the map displayed is extremely far. Then you can hit on **Active.**

5. **Erase This Device**: If the chance of recovering your iPhone is less than 50% which is very narrow, then you can choose the option by tapping it.

Hint: if you eventually selected **Erase This Device** because you have initially lost hope of finding it, as a result, you would not be able to track your iPhone again. But, if by slim opportunity you found the iPhone, you will only be able to restore all the erased data and documents on your iPhone through iCloud backup.

How You Can Share Your Location with Others

You will need to select the people that you wanted to share your location with. This option will enable you to track down your lost iPhone on your friend's iPhone.

Homescreen: Hit on **Find My**

App Icon

Find My: Hit on **People** icon at the bottom left of the screen.

People: Hit on **Start Sharing Location**

Start Sharing Location

> ➢ Type the **Name of the Person** you want to share your location into the Text Field and hit on **Send** at the top right angle of the page.
> ➢ An Optional Dialog Box will show up to select "time for the sharing of your location with the person". Select any of the flowing options:
>> ✓ Share for One Hour
>> ✓ Share Until End of Day
>> ✓ Share Indefinitely
> ➢ Notification: On a Dialog box you will see "You Shared Your Location with the Person's Contact. Hit on **OK.**

How You Can Setup CarPlay Connection on Your iPhone & Car Stereo

You need to confirm if your car is supporting Apple CarPlay before you start the connection process.

What to Do First
> ➢ Confirm the CarPlay compatibility with your Stereo.
> ➢ Verify if the use of CarPlay is allowed in your area or Country.
> ➢ Start your car, let the screen stereo boot, and show the Homescreen.
> ➢ Perform your iPhone Settings for CarPlay
> ➢ Activate Siri.

Activate Siri On Your iPhone

Homescreen: Hit on **Settings**

Hit on **Siri & Search**

: Put On all the activators.

Different Ways of Connecting CarPlay from Your iPhone 11 to Your Car
1. Lightning to USB cable connection.
2. Bluetooth connection.
3. Wireless connection.

Connection Process for USB Car Port

➢ Start your Car and let the Car's Stereo boot to the Homepage.
➢ Insert the small power connector of the USB cable to your iPhone USB power port. Ensure you hear a clear click sound,
➢ Insert the second end of the USB cord into the Stereo USB port.
➢ **Once it is properly connected:** You will see the **Apple CarPlay** icon among the Apps icon on the Car's Homescreen.

Connection Process for Car Using Wireless or Bluetooth

➢ Press and hold down the **Voice-Command** on the Steering Wheel.
➢ **Go to Your iPhone 11**

Homescreen: Hit on Settings.

Settings: Scroll down to hit on **General**

General: Hit on **CarPlay**

CarPlay

➢ Hit on **Available Car**
➢ Select your Car name.

- ➢ **Once it is connected:** You will see all the **Apple CarPlay** Icon among the Apps icon on the Car's Homescreen.

On Your Touch Sensitive Stereo

- ➢ The stereo will restart and show **Caution** information, read and hit on **I Agree**
- ➢ In few seconds the **Apple CarPLay** icon will show.
- ➢ Hit on the **Apple CarPlay.** All your iPhone Apps (e.g. Call, Music, Messages, Maps, Audiobooks, YouTube, etc.) will display on the Stereo CarPlay Screen. Press the bottom right arrow to see more Apps.

To Add More App to the Default Apps on Your Touch Sensitive Stereo Homescreen

Homescreen: Hit on Settings.

Settings: Scroll down to hit on **General**

General: Hit on **CarPlay**

CarPlay: Select the Name of your Car (e.g. **SUBARU**)

SUBARU: Hit on **Customize**

Customize: Scroll down the page and select from the Apps under

174

MORE APP by tapping on the Add Sign in a green circle in front of the App you want to be added on the Car Stereo Homescreen. You can also add Google Map to complement Apple Map.

To Remove Apps: Under the **INCLUDE** list of all the default apps on the Car's Homescreen hit on Minus Sign to in a red circle at the front of the App to delete the App from the list. You can restore it by going to MORE APP and hit on Add sign.

How You Can Rearrange The Apps On The CarPlay Homescreen

Customize: Hit on the App and drag it either up or down within the Apps. The Apps will show on the CarPlay Homescreen exactly you arranged them on the **Customized List.**

How You Can Use Siri to Assist You on CarPlay Operation

Siri is very helpful in giving reliable suggestions through the CarPlay to let you know the possible next line of actions or sending a message to someone by dictating your message directly.

You can instruct Siri to forward a call to any of your favorite contacts.

However, the type of your car will determine how you can use Siri to do what you want it to do for you.

There three major ways you can use Siri with your CarPlay.
1. On the Stereo Sensitive Touchscreen touch and hold **CarPlay Home** and ask Siri to do you it to do for you.
2. On the Stereo Sensitive Touchscreen touch and hold **CarPlay Dashboard** and give Siri instruction.
3. On the **Steering Wheel** press and hold the **Voice-Command button** and ask Siri what you wanted.

To Send Message On CarPlay Through Siri

Homescreen: Hit on the **Messages App** icon

Messages: Select the **Name of the Person** you want to send a message to. You can press on the up and down arrow to search for the recipient name up and down of the screen.

Siri icon will appear to send your message. Then dictate your message and Siri will repeat the dictated message back for confirmation.

If what you have said were correct, you can say "Perfect" and order, Siri, to "Send the message". Siri will reply to you that your message has been sent.

How You Can Setup 3D Map Guide

CarPlay Homescreen: Hit on **Map** icon

Map: Hit on **Destinations** at the top right of the screen

Destination: Select from any of these destinations:

1. **Get directions to a destination in the list:** Choose your Destination by tapping.
2. **Get direction to a**

176

nearby service: Choose Service Category including Coffee, Gas or Parking; and choose the destination.

OR

Use Siri: Ask Siri:

- ➤ Take me to the address in the destination.
- ➤ Take me home
- ➤ Take me to the nearest fueling station or gas station
- ➤ Take me to the nearest hospital
- ➤ Take me to the nearest Shopping Mall
- ➤ Find the nearest hotel
- ➤ Tell me the location of where I am … and many others.

How You Can Use Map on Your iPhone 11

Homescreen: Hit on the **Maps** icon.

Maps: Hit on **Directions**

Directions: Select

- ✓ **Drive:** If you are driving
- ✓ **Walk:** If you want to trek the distance
- ✓ **Transit:** If you will be taking various transport
- ✓ **Ride:** If you want to embark on the distance with bicycle, motorcycle, or tricycle.
- ➤ Choose the route you want. Maps will show you the shortest direction with consideration of traffic conditions.
- ➤ Hi on **Go.** For you to see the general overview of your route bearing direction.
- ➤ Hit on **Tap for Overview** in the banner. Also, you may hit on **Share ETA** to share your location with others.
- ➤ To stop the **Navigation** hit on **End** and hit on **End Route.**

Use Siri: Ask Siri to "**Stop Navigating**" once you have **Hands-Free Activated** (Switched "ON").

How You Can Prevent Tolls or Highways

Homescreen: Hit on **Settings**

Settings: Hit on **Maps**

Maps: Hit on **Driving & Navigation**

Driving & Navigation: Hit the Activator of **Tolls or Highways**

Hint: As soon as you commence your movement, the Maps will automatically update itself to show you the most appropriate direction.

The hindrance on your route bearing could be seen on Maps iPhone by using your finger to scroll up.

Maps will prevent you from missing your predictive turn at the beginning and the walking out of the route by showing you the perfect lane you should remain when you are driving.

REFERENCE

SUPPORT.APPLE.COM/EN-US

Gratitude

Thank you for buying this inevitable iPhone Guide companion. I strongly believed that at the end of the reading and application of all the working steps in this manual you would surely accomplish all your expectations and be happy with the use of the latest iPhone versions.